FEEDING YOUR
APPETITES

TAKE CONTROL *of* WHAT'S CONTROLLING YOU!

D1041840

FEEDING YOUR
APPETITES

Take Control *of* what's Controlling You!

STEPHEN
ARTERBURN

Founder of *Women of Faith* and best-selling author of *Every Man's Battle*
and DR. DEBRA CHERRY

Thomas Nelson
Since 1798

NASHVILLE   DALLAS   MEXICO CITY   RIO DE JANEIRO   BEIJING

Published in Nashville, Tennessee, by Thomas Nelson. Thomas Nelson is a trademark of Thomas Nelson, Inc.

Thomas Nelson, Inc. titles may be purchased in bulk for educational, business, fund-raising, or sales promotional use. For information, please e-mail SpecialMarkets@ThomasNelson.com.

Stephen Arterburn published in association with Alive Communications, 7680 Goddard Street, Suite 200, Colorado Springs, Colorado 80920.

Debra Cherry published in association with Yates & Yates, LLP, Literary Agents, Orange, California.

Scripture quotations are taken from The Holy Bible, New International Version, © 1973, 1978, 1984, International Bible Society. Used by permission of Zondervan Bible Publishers.

Cover Design: Brand Navigation, LLC | www.brandnavigation.com
Cover Image: Photonica/Iconica
Interior Design: Inside Out Design & Typesetting

Library of Congress Cataloging-in-Publication Data

Arterburn, Stephen, 1953–
    Feeding your appetites : take control of what's controlling you / Stephen Arterburn & Debra Cherry.
        p. cm.
    ISBN 978-0-7852-8924-1
    1. Compulsive behavior—Religious aspects—Christianity.   2. Self-control—Religious aspects—Christianity.   3. Addicts—Religious life.   I. Cherry, Debra L.   II. Title.
BV4598.7.A767   2004
241'.68—dc22   2004011514

Printed in the United States of America
07 08 09 10 11 RRD 5 4 3 2 1

CONTENTS

FOREWORD

Lcohol. Power. Money. Food. Sex. Shopping. Gambling. All are capable of causing normal appetites to become full-blown addictions. More than twenty-five years ago, I (Steve) started working with people whose appetites were out of control. Desire had literally taken over and caused ruin in their lives.

As hard as these people struggled, getting their problem appetites under control had proved out of the question. The original experiences with whatever they desired could not be repeated. Euphoria that had once made them feel so good was beyond reach no matter how hard they tried to recapture it. It was as if they were pursuing a counterfeit of their original affection. Satisfying that particular desire no longer delivered the same promise. Appetites once held in healthy balance were now losing a battle as compulsion drove these people to repeat their addictive behaviors, despite negative consequences. Their original, God-given appetites were now painful addictions.

I have been exactly where they were. I remember what life was like out of control and how I was barely hopeful of a life beyond mere survival. My first struggle was with food. Enough was never enough. My favorite women were Sara Lee, Little Debbie, Aunt Jemima, and Mrs. Butterworth. Given a chance, I would have become a lover to any of them. And that was my other problem appetite. Sex became a soothing, satisfying fix for me. I was promiscuous and loved to be loved. But no woman could fill the emptiness I felt inside. Not even the baby I created with one filled that hollow. And the subsequent abortion I paid for intensified the appetites of my heart.

Food and sex couldn't heal what was wrong. So when I started working with people whose appetites were out of control, like mine, I was actually working for me. (Of everyone, the healer is often in the greatest need of help.) As I began working with those termed "out of control," I met others who were on the road to recovery and now regaining control of their lives. These "success stories" were learning how to be conquered by nothing because they were finding out how to crave nothing. Their humility and gratitude regarding their victory was intriguing and palpable. I wanted to be like them; I wanted to possess their wisdom and be in possession of myself.

So I set out on a journey to understand what I had to do to get my appetites under control. Along the way I learned something amazing: every human being has an inborn desire to know God, but our personal and selfish wants get in the way. Our desire for knowledge of our Creator is taken hostage, and we find ourselves captured instead by appetites for foods, feelings, or experiences. We can identify with the words of the apostle Paul in Romans 7:15 and following: "I do not understand what I do. For what I want to do I do not do, but what I hate I do. . . . For I have the desire to do what is good, but I cannot carry it out. . . . Now if I do what I do not want to do, it is no longer I who do it, but it is sin living in me that does it."

Paul is talking about sin in the theological sense. Adam and Eve's desires were in perfect harmony with God and His creation. But with the Fall, sin came into the world and has ever since caused mankind's appetites to become attached, and even enslaved, to various ungodly behaviors, material possessions, and even people.

When I fully understood this reality, I realized that my choices to satisfy my various problem appetites were symptomatic of my ongoing, willful rebelliousness against God. God gave me these appetites. I am supposed to live as He intended and to enjoy Him. However, when I let my appetites get out of balance and allowed them to take priority in my life, God became distant and my behavior less Christlike.

Before now you may not have given much thought to what drives your life and why certain behaviors seem out of control—or that there is a connection between your personal addictions and your walk with the Lord. If so, you are not alone. I am one such example. When I realized I couldn't get my appetites under control on my own strength, I started down the road to healing. After I surrendered my considerable burdens to the God who created me and admitted that fixing myself was beyond my capabilities, God brought my appetites back under control.

In October 2003 I was in Cape May, New Jersey, with three hundred incredible men and women who were struggling with their weight. They had each paid nearly two thousand dollars to learn how to take control of their craving for food and no longer be defined by their weight.

When I conduct these institutes, I invite people who previously attended to come back at a special rate. Some favorite people were among those returning alumni who came to Cape May. I had gotten to know them at other events we produced, so I felt very comfortable asking them a tough question: "Initially you came to a seminar because your desire for food was out of control. If you have since lost weight and taken control of your appetite, what is your state of mind when you keep that appetite in control? More precisely, what enhances your ability to control that appetite?"

My question was met with silence. It appeared that they had not considered the driving, controlling, self-destructive force behind their personal compulsions. If you think this is insignificant, consider what it would be like to sit in the sunshine each afternoon and be burned every day for days on end, yet never question where that source of painful heat was coming from.

I felt the uneasiness in the group as each person stopped to consider the root cause of their weight problem. Perhaps you are in the same place, unsure of how to begin this journey of healing. If so, this is the book for you. But this journey won't be quick, and it won't be easy. Change requires perseverance, even when our circumstances are painful and the journey takes a long time.

Think of this book as a roadmap for the journey to get your appetites and desires back on track. By picking up this book, you have demonstrated your desire to seek help and ultimately to find healing. We want the life God meant you to live to be a reality, and we are so glad you chose this book as a resource to get there. Let us now start on the road to restoring our appetites.

The desire of love, Joy:

The desire of life, Peace:

The desire of the soul, Heaven:

The desire of God . . . a flame-white secret forever.

—WILLIAM (FIONA McLEOD) SHARP

1

THE QUEST FOR FULFILLMENT

A S UNIQUE AND SPECIAL AS EACH PERSON IS, all of us share a single trait. At the core of our being, we are all searching to experience fulfillment. Though that desire may drive some of us to look in one place while others choose a different route, the fact remains that we are all on the same journey. For most of us, our quest for fulfillment is a search to love and be loved, to have meaning and purpose, and to be satisfied with who we are.

We have been formed in the image of God with this innate need to become complete, whole, satisfied. Try as we may, we cannot escape this desire because God made us this way. So even though we might not know exactly what we are searching for, we can't stop trying to satisfy this inner void.

We spend much of our time trying to meet our longing for fulfillment. Our search for fulfillment drives us forward and motivates us to meet our needs and fulfill our wants. The *appetites* we have for those things that are necessary for our physical, emotional, and spiritual survival help fill that void.

No matter how many stories we hear about certain things in life not bringing fulfillment, we still develop strong appetites for those very things. Some choose to go after money, working and living as if their life depended on attaining wealth. Every decision, and for some, each waking moment, is driven by an appetite for more and more money.

An appetite for wealth often is an appetite that cannot be satisfied. With money, the more of it you have, the more likely you are to want even more. Having "enough," even when a person has a quantity beyond that measure, is an unattainable goal. The only people who ever find fulfillment in their wealth are those who move from being driven by acquisition of it to the charitable distribution of it.

I (Steve) have always enjoyed the television show *Martha Stewart Living.* Leading lady Martha Stewart specializes in sharing ideas for organization and skills ranging from cooking to gardening to decorating and beyond. As a man who loves to cook, I especially enjoyed the segments having to do with food. Her magazine, *Martha Stewart Living,* is a veritable work of art. Not surprisingly, Stewart became a multimillionaire for her many talents and overall penchant for doing things up "right," be it in the kitchen, garden, or living room. Yet now Martha Stewart is a convicted felon because she acted illegally during a stock sale to save a sum of roughly forty-five thousand dollars, pocket change to a person of her wealth. Then she tried to cover it up and got into bigger trouble. She threw away her reputation and will likely spend time in jail . . . all for just a little more money! A person's appetite for more and more money will not be satiated unless that person changes his or her perspective on money and what is done with it. But certainly money is not the only trap.

Others struggle with an appetite for power. It matters little whether it is the mother who insists on controlling every aspect of her children's lives or the corporate executive who cannot function unless he micromanages every detail and every decision he can possibly control. Both have an appetite for total control, which, even if they were to attain, will never bring fulfillment. Quite the opposite, this appetite produces great frustration because much of what happens is beyond our pathetically short reach. Life has too many variables to factor in or manage, even when the best, most organized control specialist works out everything mathematically.

I recently spoke with a woman who felt secure only when she was in total control of her environment. Her fears of the unknown had triggered a desire for absolute control to the point that she was no longer able to enjoy living. Driving a car was too risky and sitting next to people on the bus while someone else was driving was even scarier. As a result, this woman had shrunk her entire world down to the square footage of her house, and she had lived this way for several years. She depended on others to deliver her groceries, buy her clothes, and take care of errands that required her to leave her home. The friends who thought they were helping her became wardens of her self-imposed prison. More than anything, this woman longed for safety, control, and predictability.

Hearing this sad tale, I felt instant compassion for her. I wanted to tell her to rethink her choice of existence, to instead consider facing her fears, even if it meant experiencing pain. Anything to help her see the prison she had locked herself inside. I opted to get to the heart of the matter with her. I told her she could never make her world small enough to remove every element of risk from it. The stove could catch fire, a plane could crash into her yard, or she could fall in the shower. No matter how confined and protected she thought she was, there would still be risks and unknowns out of her control. Until she resolved the underlying reason for her fear, she would feel panic and uncertainty at every turn.

Interestingly, she was only facing this issue with control because a crisis had surfaced. She had found a lump in her breast. A home-healthcare nurse came to the house and took a blood sample so a doctor could make some preliminary assessments. The results of the bloodwork were indicative of cancer, but to be certain, she needed to have a mammogram and undergo a biopsy. But that would require a trip across town, and the woman didn't think she could handle it. So there she was, confined to her home by fears of the unknown, yet possibly facing terminal cancer if she remained in the place that to her represented total security. Sound ridiculous? Certainly her desire to control her life had gone far beyond normal limits and was approaching an obsession, but what motivated her to behave this way was really a basic desire to protect herself. Don't we all have that desire?

Successful but Unsatisfied

We can all think of both famous and not-so-famous people with problem appetites that serve as examples for what can happen.

• *Elvis Presley.* Considered by many even decades after his death to be the king of rock 'n' roll, Elvis Presley appeared to have everything going for him. Fame, wealth, women, talent, influence, and fans were his companions, yet Elvis still felt unsatisfied. No doubt he was searching for fulfillment, but instead he ended up partying all night and sleeping all day—assisted by drugs on both ends, probably because he felt empty and alone. Eventually, "The King" ended up divorced, overweight, and dependent on prescription drugs. Those exact things he was using to seek fulfillment eventually turned on him and took his life. At forty-two, he died from heart problems most likely brought on by drug dependency and obesity.

In many ways Elvis was a remarkable man. There are wonderful stories of his generosity to those in need. He had spiritual roots and a tremendous desire to know who God was. This amazing performer is the ultimate example of what happens when we live trying to fulfill our appetites—we die trying. When an appetite becomes the driving force, enough is never enough. This king had more than enough fame and fortune, but apparently it wasn't enough to bring him satisfaction.

• *Marilyn Monroe.* Another example of someone who appeared to have it all, Marilyn Monroe died tragically. She was successful by society's standards, having fame, fortune, and beauty. Marilyn lived a life of influence as a celebrity. But none of what she achieved was enough for her to stop seeking that elusive something that would make her truly happy. When she overdosed at age thirty-six, she had been married three times, was suspected of having numerous affairs, had made two suicide attempts, and was addicted to drugs and alcohol.

• *Karen Carpenter.* By the age of nineteen, Karen Carpenter had signed a recording contract that led to four gold albums and sold-out concerts all over the world. Yet her desire to be thin destroyed her life. This desire was so out of control that at one point in her career, she weighed only eighty pounds! In an effort to maintain control of her weight, Karen used thyroid medicine and ipecac to an excessive degree. Once the eating disorder was in the driver's seat, it drove her right up to the door of death without her being able to regain control of her health or her life. Misuse of these medicines led this successful musician to her death. At just thirty-three years of age, Karen died from heart failure resulting from anorexia and the destructive use of medicines.[1]

Your natural appetites to be loved and secure are not wrong in and of themselves, but how you go about fulfilling those appetites can very quickly turn ugly if you are not careful. The natural appetite for companionship cannot be fulfilled with prostitution, pornography, or sleeping with another person only for your pleasure. These are wrong choices for a normal, God-given appetite that, when fulfilled correctly, bring men and women together to marry, have families, and love one another.

This appetite for intimacy, like all the other appetites God has given us, can direct us to experience physical health, loving relationships, and contentment or illness, isolation, and despair, depending on how we fulfill it. Not surprisingly, how you fulfill your appetites needs to be aligned with what God has ordained in His Word.

CREATED FOR A PURPOSE

Let's look at what Scripture has to say about how we are made. Psalm 139:13–14 declares, "For you created my inmost being; you knit me together in my mother's womb. I praise you because I am fearfully and wonderfully made; your works are wonderful." We are the works of God's hands. *His handmade treasures.* When something is handmade, there are no two models that are exactly alike. My God took the time to knit me together in my mother's womb. And He knit you together too. Picture yourself as part of that concept. Imagine being uniquely planned, formed, and knit together by the Creator of our entire universe.

As unique individuals, we are knit together with our own set of likes, dislikes, desires, talents, and skills that work together to help us accomplish what God had in mind when He made us. Anyone who has ever knitted something (or watched someone else do this) knows that long before a person starts knitting, she must decide what she wants to make and what it will be used for. If she's planning to knit something that can be used to keep a newborn baby warm, then she is going to choose just the right yarn and pick a blanket pattern that will best keep out the cold. With enough planning and skill, the end result is not going to resemble a cute little mitten. Instead, because she knew the purpose of her handmade item, she will make it to best serve her intended purpose.

God (much more than we humans) knew His particular plan regarding our makeup before He knit together our "inmost being." Because He knew His plans for you, He placed inside you all the talents, skills, and even appetites and desires that you would need to accomplish just what He had in mind. You are unique and created with a unique purpose; therefore, your appetites and desires are unique.

All of this is to say that the things that will fulfill our appetites are going to be diverse and varied from one person to the next. Some of us have stronger appetites in one area or another, while other people may have no desire at all for what we do. Whatever you do will reflect your distinctive set of appetites and desires, whether it be:

- the career you choose,
- the way you spend your money,
- how often you want sex and what kind of sex you want,
- the types of friends you build relationships with,
- the amount of champagne you drink at a party, or
- how you prioritize your activities.

You don't need to compare yourself to anyone else to determine whether what you are doing is right. You only need to seek God and compare your actions with His plan for your life. And just so you know, if you are seeking Him first, then your appetites will be fulfilled in ways that glorify God and benefit you and others.

WHAT IS *APPETITE*?

By now you know that when we use the word *appetite* we are not talking about our need to eat food. We are using that term to describe *any strong desire we have to fill a specific need*, such as the craving for food, sex, power, pleasure, work, companionship, wisdom, or even God. Appetite is something everyone experiences on a daily basis in one form or another. It can also be our internal need to fill an emotional or spiritual void. This appetite to fill ourselves with any of the many facets of our lives is what drives us to search outside of ourselves for that missing piece.

Appetites are essential to our physical, emotional, and spiritual survival. When hungry, the body craves food, and when thirsty, the body craves water. When you hold your breath, you crave oxygen. Were it not for these cravings motivating us to act, we would not survive. If you never felt cravings for food, you would never eat and you would die.

Our appetites motivate us to seek fulfillment, but they must be managed or they will lead us into a world of regret and tremendous emotional pain. When an appetite intended to help us survive is managed incorrectly, it may become a trap holding us in a deadly grip. Until we give ourselves and our appetites completely over to God, we will remain trapped.

The world offers a smorgasbord of options to fill whatever void might be present in our life. What we choose is up to us. As you know, there are healthy and unhealthy means of filling our appetites; what we choose makes a difference in our personal sense of happiness and satisfaction. Of course what we *should* want is to pick the healthiest choice available to fulfill our need.

There are many people in the world today who have never experienced a sense of fulfillment—perhaps you are one of them. If you are not feeling fulfilled, it is very likely that one of your appetites is not being fed. The longer an appetite goes unattended, the stronger it becomes. It drives us harder and faster to be satisfied. Appetites do not like to be ignored. So what happens when a person has an unsatisfied desire and cannot satisfy his needs? Eventually that person will go in search of any means, healthy or otherwise, to alleviate that need.

Take for example the man who has felt unloved all his life. He has searched for fulfillment in adult relationships but has only experienced additional rejection and hurt. His appetite for companionship continues to grow stronger, and his search for relief from the pain becomes more and more desperate. He eventually starts seeking relationships with total strangers that may last only a few hours or sometimes only a few minutes. Yet he experiences a brief lull in the constant drone of that unfulfilled appetite.

To the person who is desperate to satisfy an unsatisfied appetite, even an unhealthy, temporary fix is better than nothing. But we know this is a lie. When we settle for unhealthy and unfulfilling imitations of what we really desire, our appetites can begin to rage out of our control and start controlling us. We will turn to sources of satisfaction that will eventually turn on us and force us either to give up altogether or to overindulge until the bitter end.

BEGINNING THE JOURNEY

As you begin your journey to a better understanding of your appetites, we pray you will learn that with God's provision you can regain control of whatever controls you. This may seem impossible. You don't want to try harder one more time. Friend, you don't have to. The reason you are still struggling with your appetite is because you know that *trying harder just does not work.* What does work is surrendering your problem to God. You begin the journey to recovery when you admit you can't fix your appetites on your own. Keep in mind that God never expected you to. To start, we challenge you to start evaluating your life and appetites right now. Take three minutes to answer these four questions. You don't have to write an essay—just be honest with yourself and jot down your findings.

1. What do you naturally have a strong appetite for?

2. How are you feeding that appetite?

3. Is what you are choosing satisfying and healthy for you? If not, what are you using to satisfy yourself?

4. Follow your choices down the road they are leading you on. How far will you go down that other road to satisfy that appetite?

If this self-evaluation leads you to realize that your appetites are not being satisfied in healthy ways and are in fact controlling you, these next two questions are for you.

1. Are you ready to give up your unhealthy appetites?

2. Are you willing to learn to fill your healthy appetites as God intended them to be filled?

We may draw great strength by studying the personal success of others who have successfully controlled their appetites. The following story shares one woman's struggle as she dealt with negative influences and addiction before ultimately finding healing. Her new life purpose is an inspiration for us as we gain confidence and begin this journey to lasting fulfillment.

"I SURRENDER"

Bob Buford's marvelous book, Finishing Well, *includes an interview with Cathey Brown, a brave woman who discovered her purpose in life amid personal tragedy. Here he recounts Cathey's story.*

She had alcoholic parents. As a result, she became a perfectionist child who refused ever to be out of control. She was determined that she would never end up like her mother and father. So she became a high achiever in school. She made top grades, she was on the drill team, and she served in student government. From the beginning, Cathey set her sights sky high.

Today, at age 54, she's a very attractive and accomplished woman who describes her journey in a most compelling way, recounting how she let herself slip for a time into the very habits she had worked so hard to avoid. Hard work, a divorce, and various business struggles eventually led her to seek relaxation first in alcohol, then in prescription drugs, until one day she realized she couldn't control her cravings. She was an alcoholic.

"This all came about after my daughter was born," Cathey told me. "I began drinking and abusing prescription drugs, and I struggled with my addiction for a long time. When I got into my own recovery, I learned about the problems that adult children of alcoholics have to deal with. I had grown up in that environment, and finally I had a label for it. But I suddenly realized that my daughter was at extremely high risk for repeating the same thing.

"I really wanted to do something to stop that pattern," she said. "I looked around for whatever was available, but I didn't find anything. I discovered that there were a lot of kids like my daughter, kids who needed some type of support group, some type of education, some type of outlet for talking about what was going on in their families. But there was nothing for them. They needed a different way to cope with their background than I had. Somebody needed to teach them that their feelings were okay, and rather than act out or push themselves to the limit as I had done, they could learn how to cope with it.

"I found out that there were some healthy things kids could do," she said. "So when I saw that nobody else had a program to give them the skills and information they needed, I decided I'd have to get involved and do it myself. I had learned it and I wanted to pass it on."

Today Rainbow Days is a recognized agency that serves children of alcoholics and others who are at risk of becoming involved with drugs. It's an exciting program with solid results born from genuine need and Cathey's deep desire to serve. During our conversation I mentioned another interviewee's comment: "You can either surrender to Christ or you can fight against the problem and turn to things like overwork, drugs, alcohol, or whatever, as a crutch."

"I would agree with that," she said. "I can think of two times in my life where I have vivid memories of surrender. The first was with my alcoholism, which gains complete control over you physically, mentally, and emotionally. You eventually lose the power of choice. For me the only way to deal with that was to completely surrender my addiction to God and let him take control, because I couldn't do it. And through my addiction was probably the only way he was going to get my attention, because in everything else I thought I was self-sufficient. But I found I couldn't work my way out of that one.

"I tried to study my way out of it," she told me. "I tried to rationalize my way out of it. I tried to bargain my way out of it. But finally, one day when I was in my office by myself, I just got down on my knees and I cried my heart out. I said, 'God, I can't do this! You have to do it, and I don't know what else to do except turn it over to you.' The next morning I woke up—I'll never forget the date, April 17, 1981—and I just had this feeling in my heart that I wasn't going to drink anymore.

"They teach you in Twelve-Step programs to take it one day at a time," Cathey said. "So I asked God to get me through that one day. He did, and the next morning I asked for the same thing. The first few months it certainly wasn't easy, but the compulsion and the urge to drink were no longer a dominating force in my life. If I asked God in the morning to help me not drink, I wouldn't drink that day. I didn't mean I didn't want to, but if I was faithful to ask for his help, that made all the difference."

But there was another threshold, she told me, that required a second surrender. "When I first started Rainbow Days I put in a lot of long hours, and at one point I realized that I was letting this thing take over my life. It was the same old fear: I had to be perfect; I couldn't show any sign of weakness. But I was killing myself in the process and that led to another turning point, both for the organization and for me personally.

"It was a painful time," she continued, "and God had to bring me down once again to the point of physical, mental, and emotional helplessness before I was willing to surrender. It was a dark and gut-wrenching time. But I went through it and came out on the other side, and as a result I have more internal gauges today. I can check myself better. I don't have a problem admitting my mistakes like I used to, and I have balance in my life."

Not only did Cathey Brown work through her debilitating

obstacle; her calling emerged directly from it. Out of the dark chaos of her addiction emerged her purpose—a work of true significance in helping others.[2]

Then God said, "Let us make man in our image, in our likeness, and let them rule over the fish of the sea and the birds of the air, over the livestock, over all the earth, and over all the creatures that move along the ground."

So God created man in his own image,
in the image of God he created him;
male and female he created them.

God blessed them and said to them, "Be fruitful and increase in number; fill the earth and subdue it. Rule over the fish of the sea and the birds of the air and over every living creature that moves on the ground." Then God said, "I give you every seed-bearing plant on the face of the whole earth and every tree that has fruit with seed in it. They will be yours for food. And to all the beasts of the earth and all the birds of the air and all the creatures that move on the ground—everything that has the breath of life in it—I give every green plant for food." And it was so. God saw all that he had made, and it was very good. And there was evening, and there was morning—the sixth day.

—GENESIS 1:26–31

2

WHAT GOD INTENDED

I N THE BEGINNING GOD CREATED ..." These first words of the creation story give us a glimpse into what God really had in mind when He created the world. The Bible tells us that six times God looked at what He had made and said that it was "good" (Genesis 1:4, 10, 12, 18, 21, 25). But after He made man, God said that it was "very good" (1:31).

It is important to recognize the place of appetites in the creation. Man and woman, with all their individual appetites, were created before sin entered the world. As Adam and Eve were created good, so also were their appetites. They had no need to focus on selfish fulfillment because they were in close communion with God. Before the Fall, Adam and Eve chose to obey God, and their appetites were focused on obedience to God. They did not struggle with fulfilling their appetites in an unhealthy, ungodly manner.

Imagine what it must have been like to not even have to think about how you choose to fulfill an appetite. Eve couldn't overeat because her appetite for food would have been under control and submissive to her primary appetite to obey God. Her own selfish desire to eat just for the sake of eating would have been squelched by her greater desire to live in communion with her Creator and to honor Him. She wouldn't have needed the comfort the food might have offered her because she sought that comfort from God instead.

Our loss of that primary communion with God made us lose control of our appetites. Blame this revolutionary event on the Fall, the event that changed everything for the worse. Our appetites themselves are not sinful—after all, God gave them to us—but we sometimes choose to satisfy these appetites in a sinful way.

For example, when we have an out-of-control appetite for food, it signals we have put that appetite to feed our body above its rightful place as a necessary and God-given function. If we love food to the point that it is leading us to put that appetite above our appetite to commune with God, we need to tread carefully because we are acting out of selfish desire. The fact that we get hungry isn't the problem; God gave us that appetite so we would nourish our bodies. He did make it pleasurable to satisfy this appetite, which we will cover in more detail a bit later.

As Christians we are called to focus on God first and our neighbor second. When appetites are fulfilled and satisfied in a manner that dishonors God and our neighbor, the act and the pleasure that come with the act are not pleasing to our Creator. However, when we satisfy our appetites according to how He intended them to be fulfilled, we are acting just as God designed us.

The Value of Appetites

Appetites provide foundational motivation. At their core, appetites serve the basic purpose of motivating us to live life to the fullest. It is through our appetites for having, doing, and being more than we are that we act to improve our current situations. Uncorrupted appetites provide ambition to achieve and make a contribution to the world.

Appetites draw people together. If not for the appetite to have companionship, humans would not hunger to be with other people. This appetite fuels a desire for intimacy, taps into our sexuality, and ultimately leads us to procreation.

Appetites sustain us physically. Food is necessary for energy and survival; therefore, God made us want to eat. He also made it possible for us to truly find pleasure as we enjoy the food He provides. Eating is truly an amazing, God-given trigger-response. We desire a food and eat, which is a necessary function of life. That action sends a response that eating has taken place and that message heads straight for the "pleasure" center of the brain.

Appetites lead us to pleasures that enrich and fulfill. Appetites that are sustained lead to pleasure and satisfaction. Feelings of pleasure, whether physical or spiritual, are a gift from God. First Timothy 6:17 encourages everyone to "put their hope in God, who richly provides us with everything for our enjoyment." Provided an appetite is being satisfied in a way that honors God, the pleasure that follows is God-ordained.

Appetites can stimulate a sense of adventure and push us outside of our comfort zone. Our appetites cause us to search for what is new and exciting. Traveling the world, playing the violin, or taking up surfing are all life-enriching activities that were likely started with an appetite for the unknown.

Appetites draw us closer to God. We have within us a longing for a relationship with our Creator. To want to know God is a quality that has been imprinted on each one of us. Our desire for spiritual security leads us to seek our heavenly Father. When we do so, we find peace and joy and love in abundance.

APPETITES IN THE BEGINNING

There are eight appetites covered in the first three chapters of Genesis. As you study their beginnings, consider carefully if you might be struggling with any of these appetites.

1. THE APPETITE FOR FOOD

The appetite for food is revealed in Genesis 1:29: "Then God said, 'I give you every seed-bearing plant on the face of the whole earth and every tree that has fruit with seed in it. They will be yours for food.'" And again in Genesis 2:16: "And the LORD God commanded the man, 'You are free to eat from any tree in the garden.'" God provided food for Adam and Eve and told them what they could eat because they needed to eat food. God also placed restrictions on what they could eat: "... but you must not eat from the tree of the knowledge of good and evil" (v. 17).

To eat and to feast is a common theme in the Bible. God created His people to love to eat, and He encouraged them to feast as a means of celebrating the blessings He gave them throughout the year. He blessed the fulfilling of this appetite in Ecclesiastes 10:17: "Blessed are you, O land ... whose princes eat at a proper time—for strength and not for drunkenness."

2. THE APPETITE FOR SEX

The appetite for sex is revealed in Genesis 1:28: "God blessed them and said to them, 'Be fruitful and increase in number; fill the earth.'" Procreation was something God commanded Adam and Eve to do. But this was no ordinary command entailing duty or work, and God didn't give it to men and women just because it would populate the world. Look at what Scripture says just before the command to "be fruitful": "God blessed them." The gift of sexual union was a blessing from God, not just a command. God blessed Adam and Eve by giving them an appetite for the pleasure of their sexual union and for becoming "one flesh" (Genesis 2:24).

We don't have to look very far to find additional verses in Scripture that focus on the blessing and beauty of the sexual appetite when it is managed as God intended it. The entire book of Song of Solomon is devoted to showing the beauty of an intimate relationship that is done right.

3. THE APPETITE FOR AUTHORITY AND POWER

The appetite for authority and power appears in Genesis 1:26: "Then God said, 'Let us make man in our image, in our likeness, and let them rule over the fish of the sea and the birds of the air, over the livestock, over all the earth, and over all the creatures that move along the ground.'" And then again in verse 28: "Fill the earth and subdue it. Rule over the fish of the sea and the birds of the air and over every living creature that moves on the ground." God created man with a purpose, part of which was to be in authority over the rest of God's creation. According to *Webster's Dictionary, subdue* means "to conquer, to overcome, to control."[1] From the beginning, we were created to be in charge of the earth and the animals roaming the earth. As a result, the appetite to have authority is understandable.

The appetite for authority and power did not end the day we got kicked out of the Garden. Some of the best examples of God continuing to direct people to use this appetite in a healthy way are presented in the New Testament. When Jesus gave seventy-two followers authority over demons in Luke 10:19–20, He left them with an important directive: "I have given you authority to trample on snakes and scorpions and to overcome all the power of the enemy; nothing will harm you. However, do not rejoice that the spirits submit to you, but rejoice that your names are written in heaven." We are not to dwell on the fact that God has given us authority or be consumed with that authority as a selfish end. Instead, we are to use our authority for God's purpose, to carry out His will as it is revealed to us.

Jesus also gave His disciples authority to use His name to heal people. "Then Peter said, 'Silver or gold I do not have, but what I have I give you. In the name of Jesus Christ of Nazareth, walk.' Taking him by the right hand, he helped him up, and instantly the man's feet and ankles became strong. He jumped to his feet and began to walk. Then he went with them into the temple courts, walking and jumping, and praising God" (Acts 3:6–8). As believers today, we have been given the same authority through the power of Jesus's name.

4. THE APPETITE FOR PLEASURE

This appetite becomes obvious when we read Genesis 2:9: "And the LORD God made all kinds of trees grow out of the ground—trees that were pleasing to the eye and good for food." God created the world, and specifically the Garden of Eden, to be *pleasing* to the eye. Why go to the additional effort to making things beautiful and good tasting? Because God created us with five senses through which to enjoy the things He made, and He gave us the appetite to experience pleasure through these senses. God made everything for us to enjoy. This is described in 1 Timothy 6:17, where we are told to put our "hope in God, who richly provides us with everything for our enjoyment."

5. THE APPETITE FOR WORK

The appetite for work can be seen in Genesis 2:15: "The LORD God took the man and put him in the Garden of Eden to work it and take care of it." When God created man, He did so with some very specific plans and purposes. As we know, when God has a plan, He creates within us everything we will need to accomplish that plan. Since God intended for Adam and Eve to take care of the Garden, He created them not only with appropriate skill and talents, but He also caused them to desire to do so. So from the very beginning, we were created with an appetite to work.

6. The Appetite for Companionship

The appetite for companionship is recorded in Genesis 2:18: "The Lord God said, 'It is not good for the man to be alone. I will make a helper suitable for him." This appetite is referred to again in verse 20: "But for Adam no suitable helper was found." And once more in verse 24: "For this reason a man will leave his father and mother and be united to his wife, and they will become one flesh." The need to be with other people, to love and be loved, and to feel a sense of acceptance and belonging is at the very core of every human being. Our appetite for companionship and love is a healthy, God-given desire. We are made in God's image, and God desires companionship with us (Psalm 135:4; Zechariah 2:10; Titus 2:14). We were created for His pleasure. Since God takes pleasure in us (Psalm 149:4; Zephaniah 3:17), it is only natural that we would desire time together with each other.

7. The Appetite for Fellowship with God

The appetite for fellowship with God was also present in the first man and woman. God created us and planted this appetite within us. In the beginning, God and humans had direct and personal fellowship together in the Garden of Eden. Throughout the first few chapters of Genesis, we see God's interactions with Adam and Eve. They spoke directly to each other. God gave instructions (Genesis 1:29–30; 2:15–17) and also blessings (1:28). Adam chose names for each of the animals God created (2:19–20). They spent enough time together for God to know that Adam was missing something he needed (a suitable helper). They worked together to fix that problem (2:18–25).

Adam and Eve apparently fellowshiped with God often enough to know the sound of His footsteps. We know this because in Genesis 3:8, after they had sinned, Adam and Eve "heard the sound of the LORD God as he was walking in the garden in the cool of the day." That sounds like a pretty close relationship, doesn't it?

Today, our appetite for fellowship with God continues (Psalm 27:4; 84:2), and He continues to call us to fellowship with Him. First Corinthians 1:9 says, "God, who has called you into fellowship with his Son Jesus Christ our Lord, is faithful." Ecclesiastes 3:11 says that God has "set eternity in the hearts of men."

The evidence is substantial and clear that we have been created with an appetite for God that can be satisfied by nothing other than God. Happily, God desires to be with us and claims us as His own: "Know that the LORD is God. It is he who made us, and we are his; we are his people, the sheep of his pasture" (Psalm 100:3). Enjoying fellowship with God is our deepest longing and our most precious treasure. It is this appetite that, when filled, will keep all our other appetites in their proper order and priority. We must learn to fill this appetite first and foremost if we hope to fill the other appetites.

8. THE APPETITE FOR GAINING WISDOM

The appetite for gaining wisdom is the last appetite described in the creation story. It is mentioned in Genesis 3:6, just moments before sin entered the world. "When the woman saw that the fruit of the tree was good for food and pleasing to the eye, and also desirable for gaining wisdom, she took some and ate it." We have already read that all the fruit in the garden was "good for food" and "pleasing to the eye" (Genesis 2:9), but the draw of this particular fruit was that it was "also desirable for gaining wisdom." Eve had an appetite to gain wisdom that drew her closer to this deadly fruit. Having the desire to gain wisdom is not wrong. Like the other appetites, it was something God created us to have.

Jesus is described as growing in wisdom in Luke 2:52: "Jesus grew in wisdom and stature, and in favor with God and men." The book of Proverbs was written for the purpose of attaining wisdom. Solomon was greatly loved by God because he favored wisdom over all other earthly pursuits. As God's children, we too must seek wisdom, since it is a gift from God.

We will examine each of these appetites in depth later on, but for now it is enough to reflect on their beginnings. Just as the world and our first parents were created good and beautiful and in communion with God, so too were our appetites. Our appetites originated not with us, but with our Maker. Understandably, the greatest hunger we will ever have is our appetite for fellowship with God. What a joy to know that we can be satisfied spiritually and have a committed relationship with our heavenly Father.

As we travel this road to regain control of our appetites, we can be encouraged to know that all our appetites are subject to God's authority. The question of how to satisfy our appetites becomes instead a call to seek to obey God in all circumstances and through all appetites and desires. That means making the necessary choices to satisfy our appetites in a manner that honors Him. When we do, true fulfillment is our reward.

Sow a thought, and you reap an action;
sow an action, and you reap a habit;
sow a habit, and you reap a character,
sow a character, and you reap a destiny.

—CHARLES READE

3

THE CHOICE FACTOR

A s WE HAVE LEARNED, our appetites are God-given and serve beneficial purposes in our lives. *So if we need these appetites,* you might ask, *what's wrong with satisfying them?* In truth, there isn't anything wrong with satisfying them. The purpose of having appetites is so that we will want to fill them! The danger isn't in seeking to fill an appetite; it's when we choose to fill our appetite with something that doesn't belong there. We may be using the wrong things altogether or using the right things in excess or in the wrong way. But most often, we attempt to use one appetite to fill another one.

To satisfy an appetite completely, you must use the actual thing that is being desired. For example, if you are thirsty, you need to satisfy that desire with something to drink. But what happens if you try to fill that craving with food? You may experience slight relief because most foods have at least some liquid in them, but this relief would only be temporary. There are many foods that would actually increase your thirst. The desired result would be even more elusive if you tried to satisfy your thirst by going shopping. These are ridiculous solutions to thirst, but that is just how ridiculous many of us are in how we choose to fill some of our less obvious appetites.

Appetites are best satisfied with the actual substance desired. They are also satisfied when we go through the pain of resolving unmet needs. Yet we often don't fill our appetites with what they desire or what we really need. Instead, we attempt to make substitutes for the real needs and experience pain every single day. The act of trying to fill a square hole with a round peg leaves something to be desired, and the same is true with filling our appetites. Attempting to fill one thing with something that doesn't fit causes our appetites to begin the cycle of becoming unhealthy and dangerous.

How Good Turns Bad

It isn't hard to see how something of great value can become something utterly destructive. Consider the element of fire. Whether a candle flame or a bonfire, this element has positive attributes. Fire enables us to keep warm, heat up food, and light up the darkness. Fire also has a purifying quality. But the benefits of fire are appreciated only when a blaze is controlled and contained. If a fire is left to feed itself or moves outside its boundaries, it can cause incredible ruin and even be life-threatening. Uncontrolled fire is capable of devouring everything in its path.

An appetite is like a fire. Under control it helps a person survive, but out of control it destroys everything in its path, including the person. An appetite out of control can destroy intimacy, scorch our freedom, and char our relationship with God. The longer an appetite blazes out of control, the more difficult it is to bring back under control.

Yet such a task is never impossible. Through God's grace and our faithful attention, even an appetite that is raging without boundaries can be reigned in. Earlier today, before I sat down to write this section, I (Steve) talked to a man who had recently read my book *Every Man's Battle.* He had used pornography for fifty years. Yet for the first time that he could remember, he had gone days without a desire for pornography or self-gratification. He no longer satisfies this appetite in an unhealthy way, because he surrendered himself to God and has accountability from some trusted friends. He has found freedom. You too can have that experience, but only if you are willing to face the raging fire in your life.

THE POWER OF THE FLESH

So many things changed once sin entered the world. When Eve took the fruit, ate it, and then gave some to Adam, their desire to please themselves exceeded their desire to please God. From that moment on, this has been our biggest struggle: the battle between flesh and spirit; man and God; self and others, wrong and right. It's a battle we fight every single day.

Because of the Fall, we are born into a sinful world with a sinful nature that wants to do nothing but satisfy its selfish desires. Our flesh wants to feel good no matter what the cost. And it's not content to feel good eventually—no, we want pleasure and we want it *now!* Our sinful nature demands immediate gratification, and the bigger the pleasure, the better. Since the Fall, we have to struggle with the reality that many of our appetites run contrary to the will of God and must be controlled or they will control us.

Although Satan had a hand in twisting what God created to be good into something bad, he didn't do it alone, and he doesn't do it alone today. Satan was not capable of bringing sin into the world; he can't be blamed for it. He also isn't capable of making us sin. Satan is only responsible for providing the temptation; the choice is still up to us. The devil has chosen his point of attack very carefully. When he wages war against us, he chooses a battlefield conducive to his plans. He wants the home field advantage. Fighting in an area where things are already falling in his favor makes his work that much easier.

The obvious choice is the battlefield of the flesh. Satan tempts us with the things our sinful nature already desires. There are times when we choose to sin without Satan helping us at all. Sometimes our flesh wants something, and we decide to give in. We often don't need much persuasion. We don't need to believe that Satan is lurking around every cookie jar, shopping mall, or sexy picture, beckoning us to come closer, to take the bait. Lots of times we come closer all on our own.

PLEASURE VERSUS PAIN

As humans, we desire to experience pleasure. More importantly, God desires us to experience pleasure. God created the Garden of Eden to be pleasurable (Genesis 2:9), He gives us all things to enjoy (1 Timothy 6:17), and He tells us it is good for us to enjoy the fruits of our labor (Ecclesiastes 5:18–19). God wants us to have the desires of our hearts (Psalm 37:4), and God Himself experiences pleasure (Psalm 147:11; Psalm 149:4).

God created us with five senses with which to experience the world that He made, and He wants us to enjoy that world. We have a particular part of the brain that, when stimulated, causes us to feel pleasure. That pleasure center, called the lateral hypothalamus, has been shown to play a part in all types of pleasurable experiences. Our enjoyment of food, music, sex, drugs, affection, alcohol, gambling, and other such pleasures all appear to stimulate a common pathway in the brain that leads directly to the pleasure center.[1]

So if we were created to experience pleasure, why not just go for it? Our society says, "Just do it!" Our friends say, "If it feels good, do it." And our flesh says, "More, more, more!" Unfortunately, when pleasure becomes what we are searching for, we will soon learn that there is never enough to satisfy. Our appetites reach the point of being out of control through the process of attempting to use one to fill another. A healthy appetite cannot be filled with something unhealthy. It just won't work. When we realize that what we are using is not working, we begin to feel a sense of despair. Insatiable appetites are often a result of feelings of despair.

Our appetites long to be satisfied, but when the chosen activity doesn't produce the desired result, we search for more and more experiences to fill in the gaps. The longer an appetite goes unfulfilled, the more pain (emotional or physical) it will generate. The deeper the perceived pain is, the stronger the need for relief. We begin to seek more of whatever isn't working. Eventually we will become desperate and reach for the "forbidden," whatever that may be, in hopes that it will finally erase the pain of despair. But even the forbidden only satisfies briefly. When it is gone, the pain returns, along with guilt and shame. Now even more salve is needed to medicate our pain.

David Sper writes in *Designed for Desire*, "The root of all sexual perversions and immorality begins with the desire to relieve one's pain with pleasure."[2] As humans, our main goal seems to be to seek pleasure and avoid pain. So when pain is experienced as a result of our inability to satisfy our cravings, we continue to seek bigger and bigger pleasures to override and hopefully erase our pain.

Most likely you know people who have attempted to fill their appetite for pleasure through food, cigarettes, sex, or alcohol. And more than likely, they are now either dead or suffering from obesity, cancer, AIDS, or other diseases. Others use drugs, gambling, or pornography to fill their need for control. If caught, they may now be experiencing the restriction and pain of jail, financial ruin, or destroyed relationships. Many more have attempted to fill their need for love and attention through unhealthy relationships that may now be resulting in abuse, affairs, and divorce.

APPETITE TURNS TO SIN

Every sin is the result of an appetite going astray and being filled by something other than what God intended it to be filled with. We experience the appetite through the sensation that something is missing inside. Then we begin looking outside of ourselves to fill it. This can become especially destructive when what we need is something spiritual and yet we are looking to the physical world to fill it. We must learn instead to seek a spiritual relationship with God to fill ourselves first. Otherwise, we will seek to fill ourselves with something God didn't plan, and we will find ourselves in the middle of sin. Harry Schaumburg writes, "When people seek a taste of heaven by their own means, they create a living hell of uncontrollable desires."[3]

We so often want to believe that the reason our appetites get out of control is that we are feeling deprived or are missing something that we think we really need. We may say, "If I just had enough money to pay my bills, I wouldn't need to drink the way I do." Or, "If I had someone to love me, I wouldn't need to be looking at this pornography." But the reality is that no matter how much we have, we are not spared from the possibility of our appetites getting out of control. No matter how much you love God, you are not exempt from temptation. We turn whatever we believe is missing into an excuse for our poor choices.

ARE WE REALLY THAT PITIFUL?

Our poor choices are rooted in self-indulgence and obsession with self-entitlement. We indulge to seek pleasure and avoid pain because we think we are entitled to it. The fleshly pleasure we seek is self-serving. All we are concerned about is reducing our personal pain. Our rebellious hearts say, *Who cares if it causes pain in someone else? At least it's them and not me.* Our desire for pleasure is just as strong as our desire to avoid pain. When you put these two together, you have the formula for personal destruction.

King David was a man who seemed to have everything he could possibly want or need. By the time he was thirty years old, he was king of a great nation and had proved himself a mighty warrior and leader of men. He was famous for his successes in battle and had wealth beyond measure. He also had many, many women devoted to him to serve whatever needs he experienced.

Doesn't that sound like a man who should be fulfilled? David had everything any man could possibly want here on earth! Fame, fortune, power, women. He loved God and was even called "a man after God's own heart." With all that he had, including a steadfast relationship with his heavenly Father, it's hard to imagine that David's appetites could spiral out of control.

One evening, David was walking around his palace and experiencing a healthy appetite for companionship. He had many wives and concubines through whom he could fulfill that appetite, but they weren't the only options available. Satan presented David with another option: her name was Bathsheba. As David stood on his roof, he had a choice to make. This king, this man who had everything he could want, made the wrong choice. His appetite for companionship turned to the sin of adultery. And it didn't stop there.

As with many appetites, once David's appetite for companionship turned to sin, it quickly seemed to take on a life of its own and began to control the choices he made and led him into more sin and closer to destruction. David's sin of adultery became a string of lies, deceit, cover-up, and eventually murder. David's wandering appetite led to much despair and suffering. His attempt to avoid the pain of loneliness through an immediate pleasure ended in more pain than he could have ever imagined.

To understand how this man after God's heart fell from grace, you only have to look a little deeper into the story. David's companions were off to war in the spring of the year, which was customary for men in those days, perhaps due to restlessness after the cold, dark winter months. But that year, the year of the most famous case of adultery in history, David did not go to war. Instead, he stayed home alone. He was not in the company of other men for encouragement and accountability. This is a lesson for us today. In our fight to control our appetites, we must remember that in addition to seeking after God, we must also seek friendship and accountability, or we too will end up with failure. Any one of us could fall as fast and far as David.

If you haven't read this sad story, turn to 2 Samuel 11 and take into your heart this most excellent example of what our appetites can lead us to.

We learn that we can feel better through various self-indulgent activities, at least for a time. "Self-indulgence is the excessive satisfaction of our sensual appetites and desires for the specific purpose of pleasing the self."[4] Our world, our choices, and our lives are fueled by our appetite for pleasure. John Piper explains that the problem "is not that we are a pleasure-seeking people, but that we are willing to settle for such pitiful pleasures."[5] The point is, we are designed for pleasure, but the pleasure that we are to seek—the pleasure that will truly satisfy—is finding pleasure in God. But we are willing to settle for mere imitations, reproductions, and false gods. We may say that our appetites are just too strong to be ignored, but C. S. Lewis gives us a different perspective with this wonderful reflection.

> It would seem that our Lord finds our desires not too strong, but too weak. We are half-hearted creatures, fooling around with drink and sex and ambition when infinite joy is offered us, like an ignorant child who wants to go on making mud pies in a slum because he cannot imagine what is meant by the offer of a holiday at the sea. We are far too easily pleased.[6]

CAN YOU SPOT A FAKE WHEN YOU SEE ONE?

When we rationally consider that what we really want and need is a close relationship with our Creator, it seems ridiculous to think that anything on this earth could even come close to imitating our spiritual desires. Surely nothing this physical world has to offer could begin to fill our spiritual longing. But Satan is a clever enemy, and we should never underestimate him. Satan knows we have a passion for worship, and he has come up with several imitations that can easily fool the unsuspecting eye. Consider drugs and alcohol as Satan's substitutes for religion and worship, and see how they measure up. Both can:

- provide immediate but temporary answers to the problems of boredom, rejection, loneliness, depression, and anxiety;
- offer the possibility of unity and connection with other people through gathering together and socializing;

- offer at least temporary relief from the pain of internal conflicts;
- erase disappointments, frustrations, failures, and feelings of inadequacy;
- produce feelings of self-confidence, self-assurance, and internal strength;
- provide us a haven of comfort, rest, and peace from the chaotic world.[7]

Satan's choices are not so far off from what we are seeking. That's why we can be so easily persuaded to settle for less. We become convinced that this immediate option is "close enough." Jeff Vanvonderen, in his book *Good News for the Chemically Dependent and Those Who Love Them,* states, "The real danger with chemicals is not that they don't work. The real problem is that they do, at least while the effects of the chemical are present."[8] He raises two major concerns regarding the working of chemicals in a person's life:

1. Chemicals are sometimes more dependable than people when it comes to helping with emotional pain.

2. Chemicals cause additional problems and pain, but, at the same time, they are capable of numbing the pain that should be signaling that there's a problem.[9]

If you are not capable of spotting Satan's substitutes for God's abundant life, then you are in danger of falling into his snares. When God offers you peace, joy, and fulfillment, He delivers exactly what He says. However, when Satan presents you with one of his substitutes, he doesn't tell you the whole story. Remember, Satan is the father of all lies. He tells just enough of the truth to get you interested and then leaves the rest out, and lies by omission are still lies.

Look at what Satan tells Eve in the Garden of Eden, as presented in Genesis 3:1–5. Satan asked Eve a question as an attempt to make her doubt what she knew. "Did God really say, 'You must not eat from any tree in the garden'?" When Eve answered that she knew what God had instructed—that if they ate of the tree in the middle of the garden they would die—Satan started his deception. He presented *some* truth and left off the rest. "'You will not surely die,'" the serpent said to the woman. "'For God knows that when you eat of it your eyes will be opened, and you will be like God, knowing good and evil.'"

Satan told only part of what would happen if Eve ate the fruit. More accurately put, he told only the immediate benefits to Eve. He skipped telling her the rest of the story. He didn't explain to Eve that when she ate of the tree and had her eyes opened to know good and evil, she would also:

- feel guilt and shame,
- have her relationship with her husband negatively affected,
- be embarrassed by her nakedness,
- never again have the same relationship with God,
- experience fear,
- go through the pain of childbirth, and
- die.

Why doesn't Satan tell the whole story? Because he knows that if we see how things will really end up, we won't want what he's offering us. This technique doesn't only work for Satan. Advertisers and marketing firms the world over now regularly use that strategy to sell their products. Replay in your head the last TV commercial you saw for beer. Only one side of the story is given to the consumer watching the ad, right? We watch the poolside scene and think, *Yes, that is the life . . . having a nice, cold beer and being with friends, all of us gathered around the barbecue. That's the way I want to enjoy myself this weekend.*

Have you ever seen an alcohol commercial showing a drunken man abusing his wife? Or the funeral of a teen killed by a drunk driver? Or the aftermath of an alcoholic mother whose children were removed from her home because she wasn't properly caring for them? Such somber ads would tell the whole story of what alcohol is capable of when overindulged.

Christians need to be vigilant when it comes to hearing the truth. Were we to examine carefully the real story behind how our choices to fulfill our appetites affect others, we wouldn't likely give in to our fleeting desires quite so easily by making the wrong choice.

Care of the soul is a fundamentally different way of regarding daily life and the quest for happiness. It is a continuous process that concerns itself not so much with "fixing" a central flaw as with attending to the small details of everyday life, as well as to major decisions and changes.

—THOMAS MOORE, *CARE OF THE SOUL*

4

HOW CHANGE BEGINS

ONLY THE VERY NAIVE CHRISTIAN BELIEVES that our struggle with sin stops at the point of salvation. That is simply not the case. If anything, our struggle with sin *starts* at salvation. Why? Because before salvation we don't struggle with sin—we just give in to it. As long as we are on sin's team, so to speak, we will have little difficulty participating in all that sin encourages us to do. Even if we wanted to get off that team, we knew we couldn't do it alone. The power that team held over us was worse than any bribery, blackmail, or extortion could ever be. We were trapped. We were slaves to our sinful nature that was controlling us. It is not until we accept the invitation of Jesus Christ to "trade up" and become a part of His team that the real struggle with our old team begins.

The coaching on this new team is great, and Jesus is patient with you as you learn to "play by the rules," which was never a part of your old team. As you struggle to absorb all you can from your new Coach so you can play the game to the best of your ability, you soon realize that old habits die hard. You know that you are now a part of the winning team and that you are loved and accepted, but it seems like some of the old team have followed you here. You had so desired to leave them all behind, but your old teammates of lust, greed, pride, and envy keep calling you and trying to convince you to return to them. You resist (at least most of the time), but their beckoning grows louder. What are you going to do?

You reluctantly decide to go to your Coach and tell Him about it. What will He think? Will He kick you off the team and send you back to that painful life you once knew? Will He tell you to just live with it? Or will He know how to fight it? Whatever the case, you have no choice but to share it with Him, because on your own you are continuing to fail. When you go to Jesus and tell Him about how your old teammates are haunting and harassing you, you are surprised to find out He already knew all about it. He tells you that this happens to every member of His team, and it helps to know you aren't the only one. The most important thing Jesus tells you is that there is hope!

Peace is not out of reach, and neither is mastery of our appetites. Healing begins with the resolution of our inner conflict between the body and the spirit. As the body gravitates toward comforts and sensual pleasures, the spirit desires meaning, permanence, and truth. The tug-of-war at times feels like it could rip us apart, but it is part of the Christian walk and cannot be traded or circumvented.

We are not made acceptable before God as a result of our own merit. We cannot earn the right to stand before the Almighty. Only through His grace, forgiveness, and unconditional love are we made clean. And only by acknowledging our need for forgiveness and being willing to give and receive forgiveness do we have a chance at the healing we so desperately need.

SEEK FORGIVENESS

If we do not deal with the issue of forgiveness, we will continue to hold on to negative emotions such as hatred, anger, bitterness, and resentment. We must acknowledge that we have these feelings toward ourselves, toward others, and possibly toward God before we will begin to control our appetites. Without this acknowledgment, these negative emotions will continue to fester and grow, and they will once again drive us toward finding some way to numb them. Without forgiveness, we will be headed right back into using our appetites to medicate the pain we are experiencing. So if you want to gain control over your appetites, you must be willing to face the pain you have been trying to hide from.

We start by admitting that we need to be forgiven. In order to see your need for forgiveness, you will have to see your life through a pair of reality-colored glasses. You will have to face the reality of how you behaved and whom you have hurt. You have to stop hiding behind excuses, self-reliance, pride, or false beliefs and start seeing yourself as God sees you—a sinner saved by grace. You are no better and no worse than anyone else. We are all in need of God's forgiveness. Romans 3:23–24 says, "For all have sinned and fall short of the glory of God, and are justified freely by his grace through the redemption that came by Christ Jesus." All we have to do is admit we are sinners and therefore need to be forgiven. If we refuse to admit what we have done wrong, we are not ready to begin healing. But when we admit and confess our sins, God does an amazing thing:

> If we claim to be without sin, we deceive ourselves and the truth is not in us. If we confess our sins, he [God] is faithful and just and will forgive us our sins and purify us from all unrighteousness. If we claim we have not sinned, we make him out to be a liar and his word has no place in our lives. (1 John 1:8–10)

To heal, we need to be forgiven. We need to confess that we have allowed our appetites to become idols to us. We have served them instead of serving God. We have sought immediate gratification and pleasure through the things of this world, at times to the point of harming our body, which is the temple of the Holy Spirit (1 Corinthians 6:19). And we have negatively affected our witness for Christ through our lack of self-control. We must confess all of these things to God and seek His forgiveness if we are going to begin to live victoriously.

After confessing to God and receiving His forgiveness, the next step in the forgiveness process is seeking that forgiveness in your relationships with others. Giving and receiving forgiveness are closely tied to each other. As a matter of fact, we can't have one without the other: "For if you forgive men when they sin against you, your heavenly Father will also forgive you. But if you do not forgive men their sins, your Father will not forgive your sins" (Matthew 6:14–15). We must follow the example set for us: "Bear with each other and forgive whatever grievances you may have against one another. Forgive as the Lord forgave you" (Colossians 3:13). If we have any hope of being forgiven ourselves, we must learn to forgive others.

Forgiveness goes both ways. We must admit to ourselves and then to others how we have hurt them. We have to put aside our pride and face the pain of how our choices, behaviors, and words have impacted the lives of those around us. We may need to seek the forgiveness of others for hurts we have caused, for not loving as we were called to love, for not letting our life be a witness for Christ to them, and for directly sinning against them. We must be willing to do this in both word and deed. Asking forgiveness means we should be willing to make restitution where necessary. Ask God to guide you as you approach these people and the pain both you and they may feel.

One reason many people struggle with forgiving others is that they don't really understand what forgiveness is. Part of our reluctance to grant forgiveness seems to be tied to the belief that if we forgive, we are saying that what the person did to us was okay. Debbie thinks this belief might be planted in children early on.

My husband, Jim, and I learned this through parenting our three children and trying to teach them about forgiveness. When our children used to do something wrong, we taught them to come to us (or their siblings) and say they were sorry for whatever it was they had done. We thought we were doing so well in getting them to admit to doing wrong and seeking forgiveness. But then one day we realized the mistake we were making.

When any one of our kids came to us and apologized for something like breaking mom's collectibles, telling a lie, or not feeding the dogs, we responded in the following manner: We would grab them up in our arms, give them a big hug, and say, "That's okay. We forgive you, and we love you anyway." This wasn't a bad response, but it wasn't effectively teaching what we really want to teach. Such a response to a child gives him the understanding that *when I do something wrong and then seek forgiveness, then everything is okay.*

We have since changed how we respond to our children in hope of teaching them a more accurate meaning of forgiveness. Now when one of our kids comes to us identifying that they have done something wrong and seeking forgiveness, we say something like, "I agree with you that what you did was wrong, and I am choosing to forgive you."

See the difference? Giving forgiveness to someone who has hurt you does not mean you are saying that what they did was okay. Forgiveness is not condoning or excusing of what took place. Instead, it is agreeing that there was a wrong committed but we are no longer going to hold that against the person.

You will very likely experience emotional pain as you work through the process of forgiveness. The pain that we must face in giving and receiving forgiveness is sometimes the very thing that stops us from doing it. We so want to avoid any semblance of pain that we will do just about anything to avoid it. But for true healing to occur, we must reach a point of being willing to face the pain once and for all, to walk back through the heartache if necessary to grieve over it, admit it, accept it, and forgive it. Only when we forgive can our appetites begin to serve the purposes they were created to serve.

The final step of forgiveness involves being willing to forgive yourself for the mistakes you have made. This may be the toughest facet of the whole concept of forgiveness. We continue to beat ourselves up emotionally and mentally for the mistakes we have made. We replay them in our heads and talk negatively about ourselves. What this really boils down to is that we have not chosen to accept the forgiveness God has given us. We need to take time to seek God's forgiveness and then forgive ourselves for the poor choices we have made, for relying on our own strength to get us through, and for putting the things of this world before God. But once we have done that, we need to let it go and move on.

When we continue to punish ourselves for something that we have already confessed to God, then we are in a sense telling God that we don't really believe He has forgiven us. Dwelling on your confessed past mistakes is not part of God's plan for your life. So if you find yourself haunted by your past, remember it is not God reminding you, because He has already forgotten it (Psalm 103:12). Satan wants to keep your past in front of you as a means of keeping you from experiencing the abundant life God promises to His children. It might help to remember the bumper sticker that reads *When Satan reminds you of your past, just remind him of his future.*

TAKE RESPONSIBILITY

If you hope to make peace with your appetites, you must realize that you are responsible for yourself, your choices, the consequences of those choices, and seeking the help necessary to change. There is no one else you can blame for the problems you may be experiencing. Regardless of your background, childhood experiences, or current situation, you are now an adult and responsible for yourself and how you choose to live your life. Does this sound a little harsh? Well, maybe it's time to get real with what it's going to take to heal and get your life back.

Not only is there no one but yourself to blame, there is also no one who is going to make the changes for you. No program or formula is going to make you change. No person is going to cause you to grow. Any change that you hope to make must be made by you and accomplished through the power of the Holy Spirit in your life.

STOP BLAMING EVERYONE ELSE!

From the beginning, man has shifted blame for his sins to others. Remember Adam and Eve and the very first sin? When Adam was asked about his sin, he shifted the blame. "The woman you put here with me—she gave me some fruit from the tree, and I ate it" (Genesis 3:12). Not only did he blame Eve, he went a step further and even implicated God Himself ("the woman *you* put here"), just in case anyone might be considering placing some of the blame on him.

We blame the person who sold us the drugs, and just for good measure, we also blame the pharmaceutical companies who made the drugs. The bartender is at fault because he continued to serve us when we were obviously drunk, and we also blame the brewers. We blame our parents for not teaching us to eat healthy, and we also blame the fast-food restaurants for providing such high-calorie food.

We do everything in our power to avoid taking any personal responsibility. We blame anyone we can find, even those who up until that point had been helpful in satiating those appetites.

It is time to stop blaming the grocery stores and restaurants for our obesity, the tobacco industry for our lung cancer, the pharmaceutical companies and breweries for our chemical abuse, the casinos for our gambling addiction, the shopping malls for our compulsive spending, or the condom manufacturers for our teen pregnancies and STDs. If we hold any hope of healing, we must start putting the blame where it belongs—on each of us who refuses to control ourselves and our appetites.

STOP MAKING EXCUSES!

Excuses are nothing more than rationalizations that we use to help us feel less guilty about doing exactly what we want to do. When our beliefs and our behaviors are in conflict with each other, eventually one or the other will have to change, because we can't experience internal conflict indefinitely. Unfortunately, more often than not what changes are our beliefs, not our behaviors.

I (Steve) addressed this conflict in an earlier work, stating that when people are "unwilling to change their behavior and unable to live in conflict, they change what they think is true to match what they want to do."[1]

Do any of these sound familiar?

- Yes, I did do that, but I have a good excuse.

- I was just made this way, so it's not really wrong.

- I just can't control myself.

- My dad was an alcoholic; it's in my genes.

Blaming others doesn't absolve us from responsibilities, and neither does making excuses. Blaming others is like saying, "I just didn't know any better, so I let others decide for me." That's just being stupid. But making excuses is like saying, "I know this is wrong, but I'm going to do it anyway because . . ."

Unfortunately this solution is short-lived because making excuses to do what we feel like doing will last only as long as that feeling lasts. Feelings change at the drop of a hat. The next time our feelings change, we want to do something different yet again. Then we have to make a new excuse or change what we decided we believed one more time.

Getting real with ourselves means taking a realistic look at our behaviors and our choices and deciding what we are going to believe. We must decide to base our beliefs once and for all on God's Word and stop making excuses for behaviors that fall outside those boundaries. The only healthy way to resolve the conflict between our beliefs and our behaviors is to start changing our behaviors to act in accordance with God's will for our lives, because that never changes. It's time to start sticking to your convictions!

Stop Believing Your Own Lies!

Our struggle is the same as Paul described in Romans 7, when he talked about doing what he did not want to do and not doing what he did want to do. At least Paul could admit his struggle. We just keep putting stock in our lies. We work harder to convince ourselves that there is an excuse good enough to make our choice okay than we would ever work at changing the behaviors causing us so much anguish.

We use everything imaginable to lie to ourselves and avoid having to make the needed changes. As a matter of fact, Christians have even used their Christianity as one of their excuses.

- I'm already forgiven.

- God loves me no matter what I do.

- God made me this way, so I know He understands.

- There is no condemnation in Christ, so I don't have to feel bad about this.

What a sad state of affairs when we start using our faith to lie to ourselves and make excuses for the sins we commit. Being Christian does not absolve us from responsibility for our actions, and it doesn't mean that we have freedom to do whatever we want to do just because we know we are forgiven. These are lies and must be addressed as such. We should never use our freedom as a Christian to rationalize our continuing experience in the appetites of the flesh. Being "free" and having the "right" to do it doesn't make it "correct" to do anything. If fulfilling an appetite is hurting you or others, then it is not part of God's plan for your life. We must stop lying to ourselves and stop abusing our freedom in Christ if we are to be healed.

Nurture Healthy Relationships

As we develop nurturing, healthy relationships with other people, we fill many of the voids that influence unhealthy fulfillment of our appetites. God desires that we live in community, and His plan for restoration includes other people becoming connected to us. Our interaction with others satisfies some very basic needs, such as our need to be loved and accepted just as we are. We need to feel valuable, worthwhile, and important. We need to experience a sense of belonging that helps us know we do not have to face life's problems alone. God not only created these needs in us, He also provided the means to meet those needs. He planned on us fulfilling these needs through our healthy relationship with our biological family and our church family.

TAKE A CLOSE LOOK

You cannot keep doing what you have always done and hope that the outcome is going to be different this time. That's called insanity. Someone who has become aware that she can't control her impulsive spending should not be spending her free time at the mall. And the man who's trying to stop drinking should not keep attending happy hour with his friends. Scripture tells us, "If your right eye causes you to sin, gouge it out and throw it away. It is better for you to lose one part of your body than for your whole body to be thrown into hell. And if your right hand causes you to sin, cut it off and throw it away. It is better for you to lose one part of your body than for your whole body to go into hell" (Matthew 5:29–30). We may not actually need to cut off a part of our body, but we should make some drastic "amputations" in our life. What this scripture is saying is that if there is something in your life that is causing you to sin, then it is better to completely remove that from your life than to continue in your sin.

What things may be helping you continue in your sin? You may have to make some minor or maybe major lifestyle changes, but surrendering means that you will be willing to do whatever it takes to get your life back on track. As you take inventory of your life, pay particular attention to those things that may be feeding your flesh and therefore keeping you from seeking God first and foremost.

Take some time right now to evaluate your lifestyle and activities, and ask the Holy Spirit to reveal to you anything that may be holding you back from a victorious life. Be sure to consider your friendships, free-time activities, interests, and hobbies. Decide if you need to make changes in regard to the music you listen to, TV you watch, movies you attend, magazines and books you read, language you use, food in your pantry, places you go, or the people you hang out with. Every part of your life needs to be open to scrutiny as you attempt to remove those things that are not glorifying God and not helping your efforts to change.

For people who have not been fortunate enough to experience a biological family that fulfilled these basic needs, there is still hope. We have been adopted into another family—the family of believers. This family can help us heal and meet many of our basic needs that may have gone unfulfilled in other relationships. However, when we have not learned to love the way God loves us, we may struggle with knowing how to participate in a healthy relationship.

I (Steve) described this struggle in my previous book, *Addicted to Love:*

> Authentic intimacy must build on authentic, biblical love, where the focus is taken off *my* desires, *my* needs, *my* hurts, and placed on the other person's desires, needs, and hurts. The joy of genuine love is not receiving but giving, not being served but serving. It is utterly different from codependency, in which I serve another to gratify my own selfish motives. It is serving another purely for *their* sake.
>
> Some people have been so traumatized or neglected that, in addition to learning to give to others in a sacrificial way, they also need to learn to identify their own feelings and needs, express them to others, and *receive* love as well as give it. Authentic intimacy involves a mutual giving of self in a way, and to a degree, that weaknesses can be shared without concern for the consequences. You become open about who you really are, rather than trying to present an "image" of openness. You also accept the other person for who he really is, not on the basis of an idealized image or for the sake of meeting your own needs. Ironically, this disinterested focus on others ends up yielding a great reward. We are able to experience appreciation, acceptance, and love *on the basis of reality rather than on the basis of a pretense.*[2]

Another benefit healthy friends and companions afford us is that they can provide us with encouragement and accountability during our struggle to bring our appetites under control. Spending time with family and friends who hold similar beliefs and values will help us to stand strong in our personal choices. The battle to control our appetites is easier when others care enough about us to check on us, encourage us, lift us up, and hold us accountable.

Man's Best Friend

Although other people are usually our first choice for companionship, they are not the only choice. Why not also consider our animal friends? Research has shown that having a pet to love and care for is both physically and emotionally beneficial.[3] People have been shown to heal quicker, be happier, and experience a sense of being needed when they care for a pet. Pets seem to be especially helpful in stressful and lonely times because of the companionship they offer their owners. Pets provide unconditional love, nonjudgmental support, and an uncritical ear. The presence of a pet in the home has been found to increase positive self-esteem, family happiness, positive social interactions, and feelings of security. So if you are in a situation where you need a little extra love and affection, why not consider getting a pet? You will not only feel needed, but you will also give and receive the nurturing and affection that we all need.

Become Involved in a Group

One final way to meet our need for nurturing is through participating in various types of groups. Whether it's a Bible study, support group, therapy group, or any variety of club or organization, joining a group can serve a positive purpose in our lives. Getting involved with others in just about any forum can help us feel like we belong. As we become more comfortable with people in these groups, a sense of closeness can develop that allows us to share areas of concern and places where we could use some extra support and nurturing. One of the best things about these types of groups is that they foster give-and-take relationships. This week you may be the one needing something extra. Next week you may be the one giving something extra to someone else. Either way, all involved begin to feel better.

FIND YOUR PURPOSE

Our appetites tend to get out of control when we focus on them and our need to fulfill them. We can almost become obsessed with ourselves and our wants and needs. The longer we concentrate on our appetites, the more likely we will become self-indulgent and focus more and more on pleasing ourselves instead of God or others.

So how do we avoid falling into the trap of becoming self-absorbed? By actively focusing on others. Having a sense of purpose that really fulfills us goes beyond believing that our purpose is to satisfy our own wants and needs. Of course, we do need to be responsible for meeting our needs and satisfying our appetites in moderation, but that is not where we experience our purpose. Having a purpose means asking what we can do for the greater good of mankind or maybe just the little old lady down the street. Our purpose is how we can contribute to society in a positive way and make a difference in someone's life. When we become focused on others more than on ourselves, we begin to feel satisfied on the inside. Filling up on healthy things gets us to the point of being able to make peace with our appetites and stop their raging out of control in an effort to fill us up some other way.

As we search and find our purpose in life, we will find that our self-esteem starts to improve and life begins to have true meaning. No longer merely surviving day to day, we can start living the abundant life God intended us to live.

While man's desires and aspirations stir,

He cannot choose but err.

—JOHANN WOLFGANG VON GOETHE

5

INTRODUCTION TO INFLUENCES

H OW CAN THE DESIRE FOR SEX BE GOOD when so much of what has resulted from it has been bad?" This is the question I hear most often from people who have read the book *Every Man's Battle,* which I wrote with Fred Stoker and Mike Yorkey. When people finally wake up to the destruction resulting from their lack of sexual control, many are devastated. Unmarried readers have their own set of questions: "What am I to do about these sexual desires? How could God put them in me and give me no way as a single to fulfill them?"

Looking at the influences we are under and what we have done to our sexuality and sex drives, it is no wonder so many people question if there is anything good about the desire to have sex. More often than not, the real question seems to be about the order of control—whether I have desires or my desires have me.

Let's take a look at the major factors that can influence our appetites and how they can affect our ability to find balance.

Biological and Physiological Influences

There are numerous biological and physiological factors that contribute to our experiencing an appetite for something. The way the body and brain affect our appetites is so complex that even those in the field of science don't have a crystal-clear understanding of it. However, there is sufficient research to explore what influences appetite and what pushes it out of control. Fortunately, you don't have to be a medical doctor or a biologist to understand what is causing your appetite to increase in one area while it might be dormant in another. In most cases, the appetite for food serves as an easily understood example of the principles that apply to most all other appetites.

The importance of the brain in influencing our appetites cannot be underestimated. As the communication center to your nerve cells, the brain is the basis behind everything you think, feel, and do. It is the brain's job to constantly monitor what is going on in the body and to seek a state of internal "balance." It does this through the use of brain chemicals called *neurotransmitters,* messengers that carry a signal from one nerve to the next, thus creating a chain reaction from the various parts of our body to the brain and back again. It is through these neurotransmitters that we gather information about what's going on in our body and receive the answer as to the best way to respond. For example, when you place your hand on a hot stove, the nerves in your hand communicate to the brain through a chain reaction involving neurotransmitters that there is danger and something hurts. Once your brain receives that message, it communicates through neurotransmitters to tell the muscles of the arm and hand to retract, thus alleviating the pain and the threat of continued damage.

No message would be sent or received without the presence of the neurotransmitters, because the nerves themselves do not actually touch. The two neurotransmitters identified and most studied are *serotonin* and *dopamine*. When released into the brain, these substances bring about feelings of calmness, happiness, peace, and satisfaction and can increase mental awareness and alertness. Serotonin has been identified as producing feelings of fullness and a reduced appetite for food. It has also been stated that low levels of serotonin may play a part in a person's decreased drive for sleep and sex.

Twice a year I (Steve) conduct a weight-loss institute called Lose It for Life. People from all over the country fly in for five days to determine what variables in their weight-loss equation need to be altered to achieve the long-term, end result of an acceptable weight. One of the variables that has to be addressed is the issue of chronic depression. I make a bold statement about depression and the proper medication for it. It is my belief that a person suffering depression will never lose weight and keep it off unless he is taking the proper medication to treat that state. Serotonin levels must be normalized in some people if they are ever to be able to feel satiated and control their appetite.

Those feelings produced by serotonin and dopamine are such that most everyone wants to experience them. As a result, people are looking for any fix to increase their presence in the brain. The search can be so intense that it becomes a craving or a compulsive demand. The substances that seem to increase the amounts of these chemicals, and therefore are things that we often find ourselves desiring to have, include:

- carbohydrate-rich foods
- antidepressants
- alcohol
- drugs such as cocaine, heroin, and stimulants
- chocolate
- sunshine and light

Activities associated with the increase of these neurotransmitters include:

- feeling loved
- exercise
- sex
- acts of benevolence and love
- the experience of beauty and art

Those things associated with lowering the levels of these chemicals, which in essence will cause us *not* to experience pleasure, include:

- stress
- low self-esteem
- hormonal adjustments
- high-protein diets
- too little sunlight for extended periods of time
- an absence of love

Any of these substances or behaviors can increase or decrease serotonin or dopamine, but we must remember that the *expectation of the outcome* has more to do with the release of these pleasure-control chemicals than anything else. The right substance with the wrong expectations will yield nothing in the area of satisfaction or pleasure.

In addition to the neurotransmitters just discussed, other body and brain chemicals also influence our appetites:

Hormones

Insulin is a hormone that triggers hunger and is closely related to blood-sugar levels. As blood-sugar levels decrease, insulin levels increase and motivate us to eat. Once eating has started, the opposite reaction occurs. As blood-sugar levels begin to rise, insulin production is decreased and the desire for food intake is terminated. Research has shown that obese people tend to have chronically high levels of insulin in their bodies, thereby causing a persistent sense of hunger.

People with large appetites for food often find refined-carbohydrate consumption is a culprit. Their blood-sugar levels spike and then plummet, sometimes sharply, which can cause insulin levels to rise and increase their desire for food. The cravings are often satisfied with more refined carbohydrates, and the cycle repeats itself throughout the day. Until blood sugar and insulin levels are stabilized, an appetite will remain out of control. However, consumption of complex carbohydrates and protein produces more stable blood-sugar cravings and will lessen overall cravings for more food. Cravings for alcohol, drugs, and even sex work according to this same cycle.

Leptin is another hormone that influences our appetite. It has been shown to decrease the rewarding value of food and increase the rewarding value of activities that are incompatible with eating. This new research shows great potential for aiding the fight against obesity.

One final note regarding hormones and our appetite for food: The reproductive hormones produced during certain phases of the menstrual cycle have been shown to increase women's biological drive to eat and also to increase their libido. This research does explain why so many women report eating more for several days before menstruation begins and their increased desire for sex when menstruation does occur.[1]

Endorphins

Endorphins are powerful natural opiates responsible for producing feelings of intense pleasure and for reducing and relieving pain. Foods with a high-fat, high-sugar combination, as well as alcohol, have been shown to increase the production of endorphins. Endorphins are also released in response to highly palatable foods and have been shown to cause a response in the brain similar to morphine. Like the neurotransmitters discussed above, anything that will cause these natural opiates to be released will likely become something we desire and crave.

The "runner's high" is a result of the release of endorphins in the brain. This grueling act of self-discipline rewards with a sense of well-being that is experienced through endorphin release. This is one reason so many people seem to become addicted to exercise, which is truly a mood-altering experience and worth the pain and sacrifice. If not addicted to exercise, certainly there are people who do become dependent on this natural high. If they go a couple of days without a great run, they become restless and irritable and all their emotions seem augmented.

This dependency isn't necessarily a negative repeated behavior. It may be that the endorphins continue to bring these exercisers back for more and ultimately keep them in shape. There would likely be many more couch potatoes who refused to get their bodies moving if not for the emotional changes and mood alteration endorphins bring.

CULTURAL INFLUENCES AND PRESSURES

In a society where the media is so active and involved in our daily lives, we must consider the effect that cultural influences and pressures have on our choices and appetites. Many of our so-called natural appetites

THE BRAIN'S MAIN JOB

Maintaining an internal state of balance is the main function of the brain in regard to appetite and pleasure. If you become overly stressed, your brain will sense low levels of certain chemicals and will immediately begin to make the needed adjustments to bring about balance. Your brain will want to make you do whatever activity has been shown in the past to release more of the neurotransmitters that will create a sense of calmness and peace. Try as you might, you can't ignore your brain, and it will continue to drive you to seek substances or activities that will bring about pleasure until it feels it has been sufficiently satisfied.

Our brain learns what it is that we do to bring it pleasure or restore balance, and it keeps track of that information. Not everyone "learns" the same things; therefore, we may respond very differently to the brain's call for pleasure-seeking behavior. Our brain remembers what has brought about the needed changes in the past and will drive us toward those activities again and again. One person may have learned to eat "comfort foods" (most likely ones that are high in carbohydrates) when feeling stressed, while another may have experimented with alcohol or drugs to achieve the same result. Anything you have associated with a sense of pleasure at some time in the past is a candidate for future use when your brain is seeking balance. *Appetite is influenced by the imprint of past forms of coping and seeking pleasure.* There are connections between events and the use of certain substances and behaviors to relieve the pain associated with those events.

The process of learning about the various pleasure sources should give all of us great hope. If the brain has learned what it will seek for pleasure and balance, then it can "relearn" new and healthier forms of activity and foods to achieve a state of well-being. So there is hope in overcoming unhealthy pleasure seeking. ◟

67

are being created, shaped, twisted, and distorted through the constant infiltration of the media. What we once would never have considered, we eventually begin to believe we "need" in order to survive or be acceptable. Without even thinking twice, each of us can come up with at least one (if not many) things we have bought or seriously considered trying that we never would have otherwise considered had it not been the advertising campaign or media from which we learned of the product.

A person with a sex drive that is difficult to control is going to be more frustrated after seeing sensual images on television. A person with a problem with a food appetite will find more food they never knew they needed to eat if they don't use discretion about how much and what type of television they watch. And anyone with a disposition tipped toward materialism will most likely want more when the advertisers convince them of new products they are led to believe they cannot live without.

The most successful ads are the ones that promote alcohol. Anyone with a problem in this area will be tempted to consume more by such ads. Stephen Apthorp, author of *Alcohol and Substance Abuse: A Clergy Handbook,* writes in regard to advertisers and the use of chemicals:

> The advertisers, focusing on our deficiencies, insecurities, vulnerabilities, and anxieties, have made us believe we are deficient as human beings. Ostensibly, unless we eat, drink, smoke, chew, sniff, or apply their product, we are incomplete or unacceptable. It makes no difference that we are all made in God's image and acceptable to him; we have been brainwashed with this pathological religion that says we are worthless as persons, our lives are without meaning or purpose, we cannot enjoy or find joy, there is no salvation . . . without chemicals.[2]

The media's ability to influence our appetites is not limited to the creation and distortion of perceived "needs" through advertising. The other area we see a major impact from the media is an even more dangerous one: *oversaturation.* The first time you heard a curse word, saw a sex scene, or witnessed a televised kiss between two people of the same sex, you likely reacted with some sort of disdain. But the more you are exposed to things that you may consider to be wrong, the less negative reaction you will have to it. If these subjects are presented in a favorable, acceptable manner, you may begin to accept them as the norm and possibly even decide to indulge in such acts yourself. Our initial reaction of being repulsed by something can change with oversaturation and move us to show tolerance, and, at the very worst, make us approve.

The phenomenon of oversaturation changing the views of the public regarding what is considered normal, acceptable, and appropriate can be easily seen in the difference in today's television, movies, magazines, and advertising as compared to just a couple of decades ago. Oversaturation and overexposure to the many vices of the world through the media has caused our views of what is right and wrong to dim to the point that today those views are barely visible at all. As our views of right and wrong change, we find ourselves experiencing appetites for things that just a few short years ago we would have run away from full throttle.

The danger is that we have exposed ourselves to behaviors that are not holy and do not honor God. Depending on our past experiences, our chemical makeup, and our relationship with God, we risk succumbing to temptation. We increase the chance that this new, sinful behavior will so alter our mood that we will want to repeat it to get the same pleasurable experience again and again. *That's how addiction starts: one seemingly innocent act or thought is repeated often enough to eventually become a compulsion.* The pull of a picture of a naked woman in a submissive act is so strong that we quickly wonder what else is available. The big win at the casino alters our mood and even our feelings about who we are. Until the dice are rolled again, we can feel like a king, an invincible winner who cannot be stopped. The feelings are so pronounced that there is an urge beyond reason to sit down at the table again. With the next loss, the need to win becomes even greater. These incidents of bondage often start with curiosity implanted by the messages of the media that cater to our desires. Always keep in mind that the advertisers in our society are purveyors of pleasure and know your appetites better than you do. They spend billions of dollars to find out what makes you tick and then entice you in the most appealing ways the mind of man can conceive.

Consider the following case. Dale never gambled because he was brought up to believe it was wrong and a waste of money. He lived near Laughlin, a gambling town on the California-Nevada border. The more the owners of the casinos made, the more they advertised. The ads could inspire such feelings that a person almost felt un-American if he didn't support gambling in the area. Eventually Dale's brain was oversaturated with the lies and promises offered by the advertising. The message was clear that no matter what was troubling you, the answer could be found at the table. So Dale became interested in gambling. Not an impulsive person, he read up on the subject and learned to play blackjack off the table. Every time he picked up the gambling book as he was studying, the subject had an effect on him. He was transported to another world . . . his legs felt weak and his skin tingled. Before he played even one hand of cards he was already getting hooked on gambling. The effect was heightened because it had been forbidden for so long. His appetite for gambling grew with only the knowledge of the game, before he had even played.

When Dale finally made it to the blackjack table, he knew more than most of the others there who had been gambling a long time. In his mind, blackjack was more like a science than a true act of gambling. Unfortunately, Dale won big his first night, which is common among those who become gambling addicts. Dale was ecstatic. Before, Dale was enthralled just by reading about gambling, no doubt a result of a slight altering of his brain chemistry. But with the excitement of actually gambling, coupled paradoxically with the anxiety over the possibility of losing, Dale soared into another world as his brain chemistry was altered even more. The pleasure centers of his brain were on overload. With his winning on top of that other euphoria, the experience was beyond all his previous expectations. Over the next year Dale came back again and again. He won every so often, but in the long run, as every casino owner in the world knows, his "system" could not overcome the odds, which are always in favor of the house. (And you wondered how they built those billion dollar gambling palaces!) Eventually, Dale lost everything and ended up with thirty thousand dollars of credit-card and credit-line debt.

For a guy who made fifty thousand dollars a year, this was a lot of debt to carry. With his retirement money gone and no other options, Dale hit bottom and thankfully sought help for his insatiable appetite for risk, reward, and a feeling of invincibility.

PEER PRESSURE

Another factor that influences our appetites is *peer pressure.* We are relational beings by nature, and as such we have an innate need to experience a sense of acceptance and belonging. Our strong need to "fit in" can drive us to give in to the mighty power of peer pressure. The belief that "everyone is doing it" has a tremendous pull on what a person who isn't participating can convince himself he really wants and needs.

Consider the college freshman who has never experienced an appetite for alcohol. All through high school, she was surrounded by strong Christian friends who desired to not drink. She was accepted openly into their group of friends. But when she moves away and starts college, she is looking for a new set of friends who will accept her. She struggles to find friends like she had back home and hooks up instead with a couple of people who profess to go to church. As she spends more time with them, she soon realizes these new friends do not hold to the same set of values that she does, but, she reasons, at least they like her. Besides, she knows who she is and what she believes, and that should be enough to keep her strong while she builds these friendships. Maybe she can witness to them as they get to know each other better!

The result is quite predictable. The longer she associates with these friends and listens to their language and goes to their parties, the closer she will be to participating in their activities. The first time she refuses a beer and gets teased and ridiculed for it will be the last time because she wants to be a part of the group. She will eventually convince herself not only that "beer is OK," but also that she really desires it. Peer pressure has created an appetite for alcohol within this young lady. And peer pressure can create just about any appetite for just about anything for anyone who needs to "fit in." Peer pressure does not create addiction or dependency, but it does open the door and push you through, whether you really want to move forward or not.

Social Cues

In humans, *social cues* are at least as powerful on our appetites as are the biological cues we receive from our body. As a matter of fact, we seldom wait for our body to tell us that it is running low on fuel before we actively fill it up. We eat because it is time to eat or because someone brought a cake to work or because we are bored. We crave certain foods not based on what our body is telling us it needs for nourishment, but because it is a specific holiday or special event.

Responding to our appetite to eat and our other appetites in general is triggered more by habit than anything else.

Cornbread stuffing, or dressing, is a case in point for me (Steve). I don't particularly care to eat any right now as I write this on a sunny day in February. But two months ago, I could not stop eating it. I had stuffing with turkey on Thanksgiving and could not wait until Christmas to have it again. And when my mom made it the way only she can make it, I went back for seconds . . . and then thirds. During the rest of the afternoon and evening, I made at least ten additional trips to the kitchen for (you guessed it!) more stuffing. A single table-spoon of stuffing probably contains three grams of fat, but I didn't care. I just could not stop eating it. Every year this same thing happens during Thanksgiving and Christmas.

There are social cues that come with the stuffing that make it irre-sistible. When I was a child, my dad's four brothers would come home for Thanksgiving and Christmas. All of us gathered around a long table for big family dinners that were full of laughter and connection. I loved those times. They made me feel like I was part of something bigger than myself. Connected with those memorable times is the smell and taste of stuffing. I can smell the sage as I am writing. It is this social cue or imprint that drives me back to the kitchen all after-noon on Thanksgiving. The memories and feelings and pleasure associated with seasonal stuffing increases my appetite beyond con-trol. But once I am back in my own home and the holidays are over, I don't have a need or desire for stuffing.

You may experience something quite similar at a church or work function. You may attend not feeling hungry at all. Maybe you even ate before you came, but before you know it, you are holding a plate full of food that just a few minutes ago you had no desire for. These are the times that your appetite is being influenced by social cues instead of physical need.

Environmental Influences

One of the environmental factors that can influence our appetites for food and other things is *temperature*. When the outside temperature is colder, we tend to increase our food intake. When it is hot outside, we tend to decrease how much we eat.[3] I (Steve) can remember my first job in the hot and steamy cotton fields of Texas A&M University, helping some graduate students with their work to produce a non-toxic cottonseed.

All summer long I suffered through the extreme heat and humidity as I bent over those plants and glued their flower buds shut so no bee or butterfly or bird could come along and cross-pollinate the nontoxic plants with the toxic plants. I lost a lot of weight in those months because I had little appetite in the heat. I felt like I was in a convection oven. The heat wiped out my appetite by midday. All I wanted was water or Gatorade.

There is most likely a biological reason for this also. In the summer, there tends to be plenty to eat when the harvest arrives. If there is such a thing as a "season of plenty," it would have to be summer. Eating becomes much less an act of survival and more of something enjoyable to do with family and friends. As the temperature begins to cool, the genetic chain seems to provide each of us with a biological memory of when food was "scarce" in the winter season. The body listens to the cue and thinks, *This could be my last meal for a while.*

A person eats more than he needs for fear he might need it later and not have the food resources to satisfy that need. If you have never stopped to consider the variations in your appetite through the seasons, do this. Many people find that being aware of seasonal appetite variances leads to better food-appetite management.

Childhood Abuse or Neglect

When we see an appetite that has reached the point of becoming an addiction, we can often trace the cause to some early *childhood trauma or a sense of rejection.* During these formative years, a healthy developing desire can make a turn for the worst. Children's needs and desires start out innocent and appropriate. But when abuse, neglect, or other serious family dysfunction is present in a child's life, her appetites may become twisted and harmful to herself and others around her.

The extended deprivation of basic needs or the presence of intense and extensive negative attention causes children to experience a sense of emptiness that runs deeper than many of us can ever know. Rejection early in life can leave a person with an almost insatiable thirst for approval.[4] This emptiness that longs to be filled may drive an abused child to seek fulfillment from a variety of unhealthy sources.

CUTTING OUT FOODS—A GOOD IDEA?

Research has shown that people will tend to binge if their diets have been restricted.[5] If a person goes without a desired object for extended amounts of time, either from it not being available or by choice, the desire will grow stronger and will likely result in the person consuming excessive amounts of the taboo item once it becomes available again.

I (Debbie) can relate to this. I have participated in low-carb diets on occasion, and for a "carboholic" like myself, this is no easy feat. I am usually successful for about two weeks, but then I have to stop that type of diet entirely. Being totally deprived of the things I love the most eventually drives me to the brink. I run for the pantry in search of the cookies, cake, and candies I have been trying to hide from myself. If I continued on such diets beyond that period of time, I would probably gain back all the weight lost and more.

At the Lose It for Life Institutes that I (Steve) teach, many participants are not aware of this information about how restricted dieting increases cravings. Before coming to the institute, they have deprived themselves over and over again, only to gain more weight and become more miserable, and often with more fat and less muscle. Some of these lifetime dieters would consume only liquids for a couple of weeks. During that time they lost muscle as well as some fat. They felt good about each day they were deprived, almost as if they were doing penance for overindulging at other times. But sooner or later a binge would happen, and their resolve was gone. There is something about self-deprivation that demands self-reward. The overweight man who becomes a fasting "good boy" can only last for so long until he is "bad" again in his own eyes. He eats destructively as a reward for having stayed in control for a while.

Due to the binging reaction many people have as a result of being deprived, one of the best strategies for managing cravings that are not harmful is *moderation*. For example, when you are on a diet that is highly restrictive regarding your intake of certain high-calorie or high-carbohydrate foods, you are likely to find your cravings for those foods increasing at warp speed as time passes. You may be better off to allow yourself to indulge with moderation when the craving becomes strong than to continue to ignore the craving and eventually end up binging on it when the craving sends your appetite out of control.

Some studies estimate that as many as 80 percent of sex addicts may have been abused in childhood. Often the victim grows up to be the victimizer, practicing the behaviors he learned from a parent or other significant adult. The susceptibility to other addictions, such as alcohol and drug abuse and gambling, are often linked at least in part to unmet childhood needs. One such case deals with a young woman named Michelle, who has successfully dealt with a difficult childhood and is now gaining control of her appetite.

Michelle felt neglected by her father and rejected by her mother. When she started getting counseling for her problems, she was only twenty-one years old, but by then she had already come to the conclusion that there was no way she could ever be happy without a man in her life. She hated being alone and felt worthless and unimportant when she didn't have a boyfriend or at least a date for the weekend.

Michelle grew up in a military family and moved around a lot growing up. She would feel like she was just beginning to settle in and make a couple of friends, and then her dad would announce he was being stationed somewhere new. Her dad was gone a lot, and when he was home seemed to have little time for the family. Michelle longed for her dad's attention but never felt she received it.

By the time she was in high school, Michelle and her mom seemed to be fighting all the time. When her mom was mad, she would yell at Michelle, "You're not the kind of daughter I wanted! You're such a disappointment!" The sting of those words drove Michelle into even more rebellion to "prove her mom right." She found herself dating the "bad boys" because she knew her mom would hate them. And even though she didn't like the things they did or how they treated her, a part of Michelle believed she deserved nothing better. Another part of her was convinced that she could change them. And besides, she loved the attention, and her boyfriends made her feel good at least some of the time.

This young woman had gone through more boyfriends than she could remember when she at last sought help. She had established a pattern that didn't waver. She would get a new guy hooked then find herself falling head over heels for him almost immediately. Her mind would be obsessed with thoughts of him. Inside she would feel so insecure in the relationship and her ability to keep him interested that she would find herself being clingy and needy as an attempt to hold him close. When the relationship would begin to waver because of her possessiveness, she would allow the relationship to become physical in a desperate attempt to keep him. This usually worked at least for a little while. But eventually the boyfriend left, which reinforced Michelle's belief that she was truly unlovable and worthless. As a result, she would hold even tighter to the next one in hopes of avoiding the pain of rejection.

In counseling, Michelle described herself as having an internal void that she knew she had been trying to fill with guys. She had reached the conclusion that no guy would ever be able to fill this hole, and now she was searching for what would. Along with that realization came facing the fact that she had been responding to her parents' neglect and rejection as she dated. In time, she realized that she would never date successfully as long as she approached it with those feelings. She is still on a tough journey, but it is no longer traveled from a perspective of neglect and rejection. Instead, she has turned to God to fill the void, and she is now living life with a sense of competency and control of her own life.

Parental Influences and Learning

Our cravings are often learned from watching our parents and others around us, as well as through personal experience and experimentation. As we grow up, we are constantly learning from the people around us. Our parents, siblings, caregivers, and teachers all affect our learned patterns and behaviors. When we watch a stressed parent turn to the refrigerator, the television, the weight bench, or the cigarettes for relief, we believe that those are effective ways of making us feel better when we are stressed. We also may witness adults using food, alcohol, or relationships as a means of rewarding themselves for some accomplishment or other activity.

Either way, we are learning from their examples that such behaviors can bring instant feelings of pleasure and relief and serve as a fix for whatever the situation is. We imprint these "solutions" and are very likely to experiment with them and respond in a similar manner when we begin to experience our own stress and tension levels increasing. We will begin our own repertoire of solutions based on which behaviors successfully produce a feeling of pleasure and relief from emotional or physical pain.

PSYCHOLOGICAL INFLUENCES

Our *emotional state* can play a huge part in what appetites we are experiencing and how we choose to respond to these appetites. It is a well-known fact that stress, depression, and anxiety all affect the various chemicals in the brain that work to regulate our moods. As was the case in the earlier discussion of neurotransmitters, these chemicals can have a huge impact on our appetites.

Depression, for example, has diagnostic criteria that are directly related to needs and desires. According to the *Diagnostic & Statistical Manual of Mental Disorders: Fourth Edition* (DSM-IV), a resource used by psychologists and counselors to make a diagnosis, there are multiple symptoms that may indicate depression:

- changes in appetite (regarding food)
- a lack of motivation
- a loss of the sense of pleasure in all or most activities
- feelings of worthlessness
- a decreased libido[6]

The presence of these symptoms does not automatically indicate depression, but it is obvious that when a person is depressed, his or her natural appetites do change.

Even more common than the presence of depression and anxiety is the existence of stress. You would have to search long and hard to find a person in today's society who is not experiencing some level of stress in his or her daily life. It seems our society thrives on our stress and keeps pushing us harder and harder to do more and more. Unfortunately, when our bodies are experiencing stress, it is the brain's job to reinstate balance. So the more chronic your level of stress, the more you will find yourself searching for something to bring pleasure and therefore balance to your life.

False Beliefs Tied to Identity and Self-Worth

People who are struggling with low self-esteem and a low sense of self-worth are held prisoner by a set of *irrational and false beliefs* as to who they really are. Regardless of what may have caused their corrupted view of themselves (childhood experiences, rejections, losses, etc.), these false beliefs can drive the people who hold to them into an ever-increasing spiral of negative thoughts that may eventually become a set of self-fulfilling prophecies.

For whatever reason, a person may believe she is worthless, unlovable, incomplete, helpless, ugly, dirty, or damaged. It is these strongly held beliefs that could push her appetites out of control and actually confirm (at least in her own mind) that what she believed really is true.

One young lady sought counseling because she had been repeatedly sexually abused as a child by a neighbor who was a friend of the family. She felt dirty and used, and he reinforced those feelings by telling her she was so ugly no man would ever want her for a wife. He told her the only thing she would ever be good for was what he was "teaching" her to do and that she needed "lots of practice." This abuse continued for several years. By the time she was a teenager, she never looked anyone in the eyes ("I'm not good enough to."), never tried to make herself look pretty by wearing makeup or nice clothes ("What's the use?"), and never got asked out on real dates ("But the boys knew where they could get some good sex.").

She was twenty years old and working full-time as a prostitute in a local massage parlor when she asked for help. This young woman actually bragged that she was the most requested and highest paid "masseuse" in the city. She liked the money she made and believed this was as good a job as any other. She had totally bought into her set of beliefs and developed a set of appetites that accompanied them along the way. Her cocaine habit was "just for fun," but she later came to understand it was really something she was using to try to convince herself she was really happy.

When we accept a set of false beliefs, they will begin to be the driving force behind our choices, our appetites, and our lives. Before our appetites will begin to change, we will have to face the reality of the beliefs we have been holding and come to an understanding of who we are in Christ. This desperate young lady eventually realized that she came to therapy because down deep inside she really wasn't fulfilled. She was looking for that missing piece and was eventually ready to face her past and the false beliefs that came with it. As she grieved what she had lost and who she had become, she grew stronger and her various appetites began to change.

CLINICAL ADDICTION

At some level, all of us are addicted. We attach our affections to the things of this world and not the Creator. We sin through our choice to love and serve other things rather than God.

But *addiction*, as the widely accepted psychiatric clinical definition of the term would define it, has characteristics about which you should be aware. A behavior is potentially addictive if:

1. it takes more and more time and keeps you from filling your obligations;
2. it continues in situations that are physically dangerous;
3. it causes repeated legal or social problems;
4. it has come to replace other important activities;
5. it causes bad physical or emotional feelings if stopped;
6. it needs more of something to get the same effect and is impossible to stop.

Even after reading this list, you may be unsure whether you have a clinical addiction. It is very difficult for an individual to objectively evaluate his situation. Addictions may be subconscious and are often kept secret because of shame or guilt. They can arise slowly or quickly. They may even have short-term positive benefit that masks their potential danger. There are also different styles of addiction. If you are unclear whether you are struggling with addiction, seek out a professional opinion.

Having covered this topic, we should note the role the brain plays in addiction. The intake of alcohol and many drugs increases the levels of serotonin and dopamine in the brain, thus causing a feeling of pleasure. Other addictions, such as sex, gambling, eating, or shopping, are linked to the same chemical reactions in the brain as drugs and alcohol.[7] It is this feeling of pleasure that serves as the "reward" that people with addictions are seeking. The problem comes when the brain's natural reward mechanism is disrupted and the person doesn't receive the sense of pleasure that the activity is expected to bring. Without the pleasurable sensation, the drive for that pleasure grows stronger. Then the individual seeks greater thrills as a way to get the reward they so desperately need and want.

Many people who are abusing alcohol and drugs or are addicted to sex, gambling, or eating may be trying to self-medicate with these activities, which induce neurotransmitters that bring about a sensation of pleasure. Unfortunately, whatever pleasure sensation the addictive behavior produces is short lived and will soon be craved again . . . and again. Through this process, people using substances or activities as a form of medication soon find they are addicted to the very thing they thought was helping them. The brain will eventually adjust itself to this excess of chemicals and essentially raise the bar for what is necessary to achieve the same pleasurable sensation.

This is where the process of tolerance and increased usage comes into play. The addict will soon find himself in a never-ending cycle with an ever-increasing appetite for the things that bring him temporary pleasure.[8]

RELATIONSHIP PATTERNS

Interpersonal relationships are one of the main ways we go about getting many of our emotional and psychological needs met. We are relational beings, and we each have a strong need to be loved and accepted. Our desire for companionship is from God and runs very deep into the core of who we are. Recent research out of the University of California, Los Angeles, suggests "that the need for social inclusiveness is a deep-seated part of what it means to be human."

The study specifically evaluated the effects of being excluded from a group and how that experience registered in the brain. The results showed "there's something about exclusion from others that is perceived as being as harmful to our survival as something that can physically hurt us, and our body automatically knows this. . . . The shock and distress of this rejection registers in the same part of the brain, called the anterior cingulate cortex, that also responds to physical pain."[9]

This powerful drive to avoid loneliness in our life can cause us to seek out relationships and then hold onto them at all costs to avoid feeling the pain of rejection. This can result in a person choosing to remain in unhealthy, destructive relationships. When relationships do break up, our appetite for companionship will intensify and drive us to find another relationship that we hope will fill us up and keep us full.

PAST PLEASURE AND CURRENT FETISHES

When I (Steve) started New Life Ministries in 1988, we began with a treatment center in Anaheim, California. One of the tracks for treatment was for sexual addiction. Men who had despaired of finding help came from all over the country for counsel regarding their sexual habits and perversions. With the stigma associated with these problems, most came to New Life as a last-resort effort; quite a few had tried other programs in the past.

Most of the men were involved with some type of pornography. Keep in mind that this was before the proliferation of Internet porn. Many were involved in an affair or had been involved in one or many before. The majority of the men who came thought their problem was that they were "super males" with a sex drive beyond what others experienced, thereby forcing their appetites for sex out of control.

Some of the men had some very interesting fetishes. One man had felt neglected by his mother and when she was away he would go into her drawer, pull out her stockings, and comfort himself by rubbing her stockings against his face. As he got older, his comfort process progressed to masturbation with the stockings. As he grew up, the pleasure of the stockings never left him. If a woman was present, he was aroused just by the sight of her stocking-covered legs. The view sent him into a different realm of thinking. He would become obsessed with her and her legs. All he wanted to do was touch her stockings to his face. He didn't need to touch the stockings with his hands, interestingly enough.

His obsession drove him into a ritual of seduction in order to feel her stockings and experience the comfort and release he had felt when he was a child. He propositioned many women—not to have sex, but to allow him to put his cheek on their leg. When one woman at work complained about his awkward advances, others came forward and an intervention was conducted. He was told to seek help for "emotional problems." During treatment, he finally learned the connection between sex drive, the stockings, and his mom's neglect. He grieved the lack of her presence and support. He saw the fetish for what it was and began to discover other ways of being comforted and feeling pleasure. In the end, with much work and great difficulty, this strange appetite was brought under control.

Early experiences with comfort-producing substances and behaviors can lead to excessive adult appetites. The link is direct in many cases, like the one above, but it can also be indirect. Often the abused woman craves food as an indirect reaction to the abuse. While food has nothing to do with the abuse, it puts weight on her body that provides protection and repels men rather than attracting them. Resolving the intense pain and anger surrounding the abuse can be the key to bringing the appetite back under control. The imprints of childhood can be treated in most cases to release the person from the driving forces of the appetite.

Spiritual Influences

"For the sinful nature desires what is contrary to the Spirit, and the Spirit what is contrary to the sinful nature . . . so that you do not do what you want" (Galatians 5:17). This is the dilemma that, unfortunately, all of us live with. Desiring what is not beneficial to us leads to potentially addictive behavior. Our natural desires grow out of control, and we crave what is of the world and not beneficial to the soul. Because we are made up of both flesh and spirit, we are constantly fighting our own internal war between these two forces. Our flesh will drive us to some particular appetites, whereas our spirit desires a totally different set of longings. No matter how much we may want to partake in a specific appetite, we will often find ourselves doing just the opposite. Paul knew exactly how that tug-of-war felt. He wrote, "I have the desire to do what is good, but I cannot carry it out. For what I do is not the good I want to do; no, the evil I do not want to do—this I keep on doing" (Romans 7:18–19). The desires that rage within us are obviously influenced by the spiritual world.

The presence of the Holy Spirit in our lives will call us toward a set of appetites that are wholesome and edifying. He will give us the strength and desire to overcome unhealthy appetites and replace them with holy ones. Galatians 5:16 says, "Live by the Spirit, and you will not gratify the desires of the sinful nature." The more we grow in our relationship with God, the more we will find ourselves hungering and thirsting after righteousness—and being drawn to appetites that really fill us up. However, the Holy Spirit is not the only spiritual influence hoping to impact our appetites.

Satan "prowls around like a roaring lion looking for someone to devour" (1 Peter 5:8). One way he "devours" is by tempting us to give in to the desires of the flesh and the things of this world that he controls. Satan doesn't simply want us to partake in the things of this world; he wants us to binge on them. Although the devil cannot actually make us do anything, he is the master deceiver and has at his disposal the power to tempt us.

We can gradually become deceived to the point of deciding that whatever it is we are wanting really is okay for us to indulge in. And that's just the first step. He wants us to take healthy appetites and make them our obsessions. He wants to then take our obsessions and make them addictions. And once there is an addiction, he wants to use it to completely control and destroy our lives.

One of the most powerful spiritual influences is guilt. Guilt is not just an emotion; it is a spiritual state that can drive our appetites and push us toward addiction. If we do not accept the Lord's offer of forgiveness, we will either be wracked by guilt or we will turn off our consciences to eliminate it. Research with alcoholics suggests there are frequent incidences of out-of-control behavior that leave the drinker in a deep pool of guilt. The one thing he said he would never do is eventually done. The line that was never to be crossed is finally breached. The alcoholic finds it difficult to live with himself. But rather than avoid the behavior that led to the offense, the feelings of guilt and shame drive the person to find relief. He seeks that relief from the most reliable source he knows: alcohol. Trying harder to be good only leads to more negative consequences, until the alcoholic finally surrenders.

In Summary

Our innate rebelliousness against God couples with the many factors that can and do influence our various appetites to make controlling these cravings more than difficult. But do not despair, because we have a great hope. For good or bad, you have "trained" your brain, whether you realized it at the time or not, to crave the specific things it does. Your brain now needs to be retrained—not an easy task, but not impossible either. Let us reflect on these words from Mark 10:24–27 as we continue the journey:

The disciples were amazed at his words. But Jesus said again, "Children, how hard it is to enter the kingdom of God! It is easier for a camel to go through the eye of a needle than for a rich man to enter the kingdom of God."

The disciples were even more amazed, and said to each other, "Who then can be saved?"

Jesus looked at them and said, "With man this is impossible, but not with God; all things are possible with God."

The desire of power in excess caused the angels to fall,
the desire of knowledge in excess caused man to fall.

—Francis Bacon

6

FILLING THE VOID
(TIMES EIGHT)

G OD WANTS US TO BE FULFILLED AND SATISFIED. He
wants us to be successful in controlling our appetites and
meeting our needs without excess. And we can be satisfied,
if we faithfully commit to follow His leading. Keep this truth in mind
as we delve into the eight appetites outlined in chapter 2.

1. APPETITE FOR FELLOWSHIP WITH GOD

When God created humans, He left a place inside us empty and
yearning to be filled with the love and fellowship of our Creator. By
doing this, God created a need for Himself. This desire should drive
us toward a relationship with the Almighty that will make us whole.
Because we sense that something is missing inside, we will go in
search of the missing piece. Unfortunately, before many people find
God, they find substitutes that they then use to fill that God-given

void as best they can. As Christians, we know intellectually that this won't work, but that doesn't stop us from trying.

Until we seek, find, and accept a relationship with God, we will long to fill that space and probably have our passions stirred by something else. Romans 1:18–31 tells us that God makes Himself known to men. However, "although they knew God, they neither glorified him as God nor gave thanks to him, but their thinking became futile and their foolish hearts were darkened. . . . They exchanged the truth of God for a lie, and worshiped and served created things rather than the Creator" (vv. 21, 25). What we don't realize is that there are serious consequences if we choose not to seek God first. Ezekiel 23:35 says, "Therefore this is what the Sovereign LORD says: Since you have forgotten me and thrust me behind your back, you must bear the consequences of your lewdness and prostitution."

When we attempt to put something, anything in the place that only God is to hold, we are committing the sin of idolatry. "Anything beside God to which we turn, positive or negative, in order to find life, value, and meaning is idolatry: money, property, jewels, sex, clothes, church building, educations, degrees, anything."[1]

Are we saying that having or enjoying any of these things is idolatry? Of course not. Idolatry is not about *what* you seek or have, it's about *why* you seek it. Are you seeking these things as a substitute for God? Are you expecting them to fill you up, make you valuable, give you security, or bring you love? If you are, then you are deeply entrenched in the sin of idolatry and need to rectify that situation by putting God back in His place of priority. If you don't, you will continue to seek the things of this world to fill your appetite for God and you will continue to feel empty.

Any appetite that goes unsatisfied will grow stronger. This is true for the need for fellowship with God. Therefore, if you try to fill this need with something that doesn't quite work, then the need continues to grow and the void grows larger. The larger the pain, the larger the next thing you will have to find to attempt to fill this ever-growing, gnawing need. Can you see how this will begin to impact all the other appetites? You will search through the methods of filling your different appetites until you find something that relieves the pain for a while. But when the pain returns you will have to search again, this time for something you believe will bring you more lasting pleasure than whatever you tried last time. And the cycle begins. We believe that unless you learn to fill this need for God first, you can expect all your other appetites to be out of balance.

2. Appetite for Pleasure

The next strongest desire that affects most all of the others is our appetite for pleasure. Other than our desire for God, the appetite for pleasure is the creed by which we as human beings live. Whatever we choose to fill our appetites with is supposed to bring us pleasure. We actively proceed throughout our lives with this motto plastered across our foreheads: *Seek Pleasure; Avoid Pain!* We want to experience a sense of pleasure in everything we think, feel, and do. We want our relationships to be pleasurable. We want our jobs to be pleasurable. We want our recreation to be pleasurable. We want our food to be pleasurable. And we even want our death to be pleasurable. We want to live in an enchanted world where everything is rosy and beautiful and where we are never wanting for anything.

Now in reality we know a perfectly pleasurable life is an impossible dream, but it is still what we are hoping for. Because we do live in the real world, we will from time to time experience pain. But when this happens, we will immediately begin searching for something to relieve the pain and move us back to the pleasure we so desperately need. As I (Steve) have said in my book *Addicted to Love,*[2] we have become self-absorbed and obsessed with our own pain. We want to avoid pain and seek pleasure, and the deeper the perceived pain, the stronger the need for release through some form of pleasure. Eventually, our normal pleasures no longer do the trick, and a more "forbidden" pleasure becomes necessary to escape the pain. We move easily from natural and healthy pleasures to affairs, illicit sex, spending beyond measure, or drugs when normal or more accepted pleasures just don't cut it any more. These behaviors serve us in some very significant ways.

- They provide relief or diversion from pain.
- They provide temporary escape from reality.
- There is a sense of security because at least this is a "known."
- They provide instant gratification.

Our society constantly encourages us to indulge our desire for pleasure, and we seem to blindly fall in line to get our daily fix of pleasure. Society says, "If it feels good, do it!" And we do.

3. APPETITE FOR FOOD

As the obesity rates continue to rise year after year, it is obvious that we are excessively indulging our appetite for food. When this appetite becomes out of control, it can threaten just about every aspect of our lives. Yet no matter how hard we try, we cannot fill our spiritual or emotional space with physical food. We yearn for a type of filling up that food will not satisfy. People today are using food as a way to escape the pain in their lives. They may be feeling emotional pain from a relationship breakup, psychological pain of depression or anxiety, or any one of millions of other pains. Regardless of the type of pain, we use food as the medicine that we need to relieve the pain.

Emotional eating happens when we eat in response to stress, boredom, depression, anxiety, or other emotional sensation rather than because we are experiencing true physical hunger.

Eating when we are not hungry can still cause a sensation of pleasure. Certain foods can actually cause the brain to release chemicals that bring about intense feelings of pleasure. So if you are stressed and use food as your medication and indulge in "comfort foods," you really may feel better, at least for a little while. But then the pain comes back. And this time it has company. It brought along feelings of guilt and shame as a result of your eating when you didn't really need it. And how will you get rid of these painful feelings? You will probably take more "medicine," right? Before you know it you have to sit down and eat an entire box of macaroni and cheese all by yourself just to begin to feel a little better. The Bible tells us our appetite for food will never be satisfied: "All man's efforts are for his mouth, yet his appetite is never satisfied" (Ecclesiastes 6:7).

4. APPETITE FOR SEX

God created sex to feel good. And because He did, He also had to give many commandments and instructions regarding it. God knew how easily this appetite could become distorted and destructive. Over and over in Scripture, God describes what should and should not be involved in the healthy fulfilling of our sexual appetite. But because of our sinful nature, many people are drawn into sins of sexual immorality. The world's view that "if it feels good, do it," and "free love" have brought a whole series of sexually related consequences upon our world, such as the increasing rates of STDs, AIDS, teen pregnancies, abortions, unwed mothers, and broken marriages. Sexual addictions, lust, pornography, homosexuality, and prostitution are all related to our feeble attempts to make ourselves happy by perverting the blessing of sex that God provided us with. Ecclesiastes teaches that sexual gratification can become a snare with chains worse even than death (7:25–26).

People often resort to using sex as a means of controlling the emotional pain and fear of aloneness. At first this may seem to work. As I explained in my book *Addicted to Love,* "The mood change brought on by orgasm kills the pain and provides a momentary sense of being 'normal' again, of being 'in control.' But as the addictive cycle continues there comes a time when after the relief, the pain returns worse than before, triggering a need for more relief, causing more pain, and so on, until sex controls the individual, not the other way around."[3]

5. APPETITE FOR AUTHORITY AND POWER

We live in a power-hungry society. It's like a great big game of "King of the Mountain," and we won't stop until we are at the top of that hill. Being at the top means you are king of the whole mountain and you have the authority to rule over all your little subjects who are weak and inferior to you.

This drive for power and authority can become all-consuming for some people. While they are climbing their way to the top, they seem to not really care who they step on or walk over. The only reason they even want other people around is to use them as stepping stones to move themselves closer to the peak. Yet these power-hungry individuals need the rest of us around once they have made it to the top. What good would it be to be king if you had no subjects?

When the appetite for power gets out of control, people will begin to use their position as well as other people to get what they want. They become consumers of people instead of consumers of things. The lives of the people around such power mongers have come under the jurisdiction of this self-proclaimed god. Ecclesiastes says this control and extortion of others will eventually only bring the one in power more hurt and pain (Ecclesiastes 7:7; 8:9).

6. APPETITE FOR WORK

The problem isn't your willingness to work hard; it's your working hard for the wrong reasons that causes this appetite to rage out of control. Again it comes down to using one appetite as an attempt to fill another. When you are compulsively working for the purpose of fulfilling your desire for pride, power, or possessions, then it's time to reconsider what life is really all about. Ecclesiastes gives a powerful

It is interesting to analyze how people use their power. Because I (Steve) take at least thirty trips a year, I stay in a lot of hotels. I always ask to be upgraded to a better room at no charge. I have nothing to lose unless I can't stand to hear the word no.

Most of the time, the person behind the desk can honor my request. It all depends on whether the hotel has better rooms available and if the person I ask has the authority to change my reservation. I always find it amusing to guess how they will use their power. Some will do their utmost to ensure I do *not* get anything better than the room I signed up to stay in. I always imagine that if they ever run something big they will use their power only for selfish gain. And then there are hotel staff members who use their authority to give me an upgraded room so I will be more comfortable and because they want me, the customer, to be happy. Try this exercise sometime. You never know—you could get a suite for your trouble and study this appetite at the same time!

account of what happens when work becomes your life. Let's take it straight from the words of Ecclesiastes 2:18–23.

> I hated all the things I had toiled for under the sun, because I must leave them to the one who comes after me. And who knows whether he will be a wise man or a fool? Yet he will have control over all the work into which I have poured my effort and skill under the sun. This too is meaningless. So my heart began to despair over all my toilsome labor under the sun. For a man may do his work with wisdom, knowledge and skill, and then he must leave all he owns to someone who has not worked for it. This too is meaningless and a great misfortune. What does a man get for all the toil and anxious striving with which he labors under the sun? All his days his work is pain and grief; even at night his mind does not rest. This too is meaningless.

It is good to be willing to work for your keep and to stay busy. There are many scriptures about avoiding laziness and idle hands. Proverbs 10:4 tells us, "Lazy hands make a man poor, but diligent hands bring wealth" (See also 12:24, 19:15, 21:25–26, 24:30–34, and 2 Thessalonians 3:10 about how a good worker will be rewarded). But we were never expected to become workaholics. Scripture also clearly states that God rested on the seventh day (Genesis 2:2). We too are commanded to *not* work on the Sabbath (Exodus 20:8–11). Jesus took time to rest while here on earth (Mark 4:38, 6:31; and John 4:6). If anyone had reason to be a workaholic, it was Jesus. He had an impossible job ahead of him and a deadline that no human could possibly meet. He knew that he only had three years to totally change the whole world, and yet he took time to rest.

The appetite for work is hard to manage because it looks noble even when it is grossly out of control. The hard worker looks good to the community, but when you talk to his family members who are living their lives all alone, it isn't so very appealing. A workaholic can have a life story equally as devastating as that of an alcoholic.

Are you using work as a way to fill yourself up on the inside? Have you determined that your sense of worth and value depend on your job performance? Do you find your sense of security being tied to money, career, or other things that work gathers for you? If you find yourself answering yes to any of these questions, then it's likely that work has become your god.

7. Appetite for Companionship

As with all the other appetites that move out from under God's original plan, the appetite for companionship can turn into an idolatrous relationship. We have been created with a strong need and desire for relationships with other people. In the New Testament, we are told not to forsake the assembling together of believers (Hebrews 10:25). God knew that we would want to be around people; and if we don't choose to be around other believers, who will we choose to be with? Obviously nonbelievers. There are several times in the Old Testament where God instructs the people of Israel to avoid spending too much time with pagans because He knew how easily they could be drawn away from Him. Our appetite for companionship can become destructive as a result of our choices of the people we surround ourselves with. Because of our strong need to belong and feel accepted, choosing to spend time with unhealthy people will eventually begin to influence our thoughts, beliefs, and actions. We will start to be more like them and doing the same types of things they do. This is the power of peer pressure at work.

Our appetite for companionship can also change from being a healthy desire to be with people to a force that keeps us trapped in unhealthy relationships. The relationships we find ourselves in may have become destructive through the presence of physical, verbal, or emotional abuse. Or our need for attention and acceptance from others may have become so strong that we have become codependent in our relationships. Either way, we are no longer in control of our appetite for companionship. Instead, our appetite is controlling us. Our desire for a relationship has become so out of control that we are willing to accept anything—even an unhealthy and destructive relationship—in hope of filling that need. We have convinced ourselves that something is better than nothing no matter how bad that "something" is for us. The fear of being alone, rejected, hurt, or unloved can be so strong that it traps us in a relationship that actually may make us feel alone, rejected, hurt, and unloved.

Our fear of pain through rejection, abandonment, and loneliness keeps us willing to experience the pain of being unfulfilled in a relationship. In this case we seem to be choosing the lesser of two evils. We accept the pain of an unfulfilling or harmful relationship because it at least provides us with the façade of belonging and being accepted. We convince ourselves and maybe the world around us that we are somebody special because we are in a relationship. Leaving that relationship would force us to face our belief that we really are worthless and unlovable. There would not be a shelter to hide from our pain.

Being needed creates relationships between overly responsible people (the one who needed to be needed) and under-responsible people (those who want someone else to care for them). Although this combination is extremely unhealthy, it has been shown to be very stable. Each of the people involved in this type of relationship is more focused on meeting his or her own selfish needs than in serving the other. Even the person who is seemingly doing everything for his spouse is being selfish. How? When you examine the motives behind the actions, you will see that he is not being a servant as Christ would request us to be, but is actually serving only for the selfish purpose of meeting his own need to feel important and valuable. As long as the relationship continues to provide for each a satisfaction of his selfish desires, it will remain intact and stable.

8. Appetite for Wisdom

When we seek wisdom, it is not the knowledge or even the desire to attain knowledge and wisdom that is of concern. Only when our desire to gain wisdom reaches the point of overindulgence, obsession, or misdirection should we become concerned. When our desire to

WHAT IS A CODEPENDENT RELATIONSHIP?

One person is dependent on the other to do what he/she should be doing for him/herself. While the other spouse is codependent (also dependent) on the relationship as a means to getting his/her sense of well-being and importance met.

Most often we hear the term *codependent* in reference to relationships that involve one person being an alcoholic or drug abuser. The chemically dependent spouse is "dependent" on a drug of some sort to get their "highs." However, the codependent spouse is "dependent" on the other person for their "highs." Their drive or appetite is to "fix" other people or be seen as a helpless but persevering victim—this makes them feel important, needed, and even "high," in a sense of the word. The codependent's mood is determined by his/her ability to "fix" the other spouse. When the spouse shows improvement, they get "high"; when the spouse fails or relapses, they experience a low. It is their drive to get their next fix, just as the addict dreams of his or her next high, that keeps them both going back for more.

In the case of a codependent relationship, both members have set up idols for themselves. The dependent person's idol is alcohol, drugs, sex, gambling, or any other behavior that has taken the place of God in their seeking fulfillment; the codependent person's idol is the other person through whom they receive their sense of worth. Jeff Vanvonderen explains:

> A codependent person turns to something other than God as his source of well-being. If another human being is your false god, you do not want a broken god who is drunk, irresponsible, and causes embarrassment. You want a sober and responsible god, one that will cause you to feel proud.
>
> Therefore, you must fix your god, which is why so much time and energy, his own and other people's, is spent by the codependent trying to fix the chemically dependent person. That is also why it is so difficult for the codependent to let go, even though the efforts are proving to be useless.[4]

pursue wisdom is stronger than our desire to pursue the One who gives wisdom, then knowledge has become our god. If we desire wisdom and knowledge so we may benefit others, it is being used for a godly purpose. But beware of using this appetite to make yourself look good or make someone else look bad.

Let's again turn to the teachings of Scripture in the book of Ecclesiastes:

- "For with much wisdom comes much sorrow; the more knowledge, the more grief" (1:18).
- "Do not be overrighteous, neither be over wise" (7:16).
- "Of making many books there is no end, and much study wearies the body" (12:12).

These verses show that an excessive desire for knowledge can bring problems. Overindulgence in the study of anything, even religious topics, can distract us from the really important issues. Second Timothy 3 says that in the last days, people will have "a form of godliness but denying its power . . . always learning but never able to acknowledge the truth" (vv. 5, 7). In today's world with all the information you could ever imagine right at your fingertips through the Internet, our desire for wisdom can be even more difficult to control. How many of us have spent hours and hours in front of our computers researching some "important" topic? We are not saying that the Internet or the knowledge you can gain from it is wrong. But it must be managed and controlled and used only for purposes that would be pleasing to God.

Now that we have studied these eight appetites in closer detail, it is time to turn our attention to the next step—the healing process. God's desire for us to be in control of our appetites is real and powerful, and we may find healing if we seek to do His will, utilizing the good gifts He has given us.

Faith is the one power against which fear cannot stand.

Day by day, as you fill your mind with faith, there will ultimately be no room left for fear. This is the one great fact that no one should forget.

Master faith and you will automatically master fears.

—NORMAN VINCENT PEALE,
THE POWER OF POSITIVE THINKING

7

FRUIT IN
ALL ITS FORMS

A S CHRISTIANS, we have a secret power that very few utilize:
The *power of the Holy Spirit* living within us. When Jesus was
leaving this earth, He promised that the Holy Spirit would be
sent here to help His disciples and us. "But the Counselor, the Holy
Spirit, whom the Father will send in my name, will teach you all things
and will remind you of everything I have said to you" (John 14:26).

When we accept Jesus as our Lord and Savior, we receive the gift
of the Holy Spirit. Through the presence of the Holy Spirit, we are
"sealed" and belong to Jesus Christ; therefore, Satan has no authority over us (Ephesians 1:13–14; Acts 2:38). Through the presence of
the Holy Spirit, we also receive wisdom, encouragement, power, and
strength to help us as we battle (Acts 1:8; Acts 9:31; Ephesians 1:17).
When we face trials and difficulties in our lives, Jesus tells us that the
Holy Spirit is there to help us know how to handle the situation
(Mark 13:11; Luke 12:11–12).

Because the Holy Spirit lives in us, we can and are to exhibit the fruit of the Spirit. *Fruit* is defined by Webster as "the seed-bearing part of a plant."[1] It is the end result of what the source or plant is trying to produce. In Scripture, the fruit of the Spirit is the end result of what the Holy Spirit is trying to produce in us. As the Spirit grows within us, we begin to produce good fruit as described in Galatians 5:22: "But the fruit of the Spirit is love, joy, peace, patience, kindness, goodness, faithfulness, gentleness and self-control." What grows out of a plant or other source will reflect the source itself. We all know that an apple grows from an apple tree, not a tomato plant. Although there may be some similarities between an apple and a tomato, they are not the same and you know which came from where.

Likewise, you will know which fruit comes from the Holy Spirit and which does not. Scripture confirms this: "By their fruit you will recognize them. Do people pick grapes from thornbushes, or figs from thistles? Likewise every good tree bears good fruit, but a bad tree bears bad fruit. A good tree cannot bear bad fruit, and a bad tree cannot bear good fruit. . . . Thus, by their fruit you will recognize them" (Matthew 7:16–18, 20). So the fruit is representative of the source from whence it came.

The Power of "Forbidden Fruit"

Satan uses forbidden fruit as his imitation of God's fruit. He uses it to entice us and move us away from God and His provisions for our life. God forbids certain things in the physical world because of the destruction they can cause in both the physical and spiritual realms. We can choose to pursue a forbidden fruit, but we need to be aware that there are consequences to doing so, such as its effect on our physical bodies, our relationships, our finances, etc. Choosing to partake of forbidden fruit can also have consequences in the spiritual realm:

sin separates us from God, sin leads to spiritual death, and sin affects our witness to others for Christ.

So why did God allow forbidden fruit? Because of free will. God wants us to choose to love and follow Him. That could only be accomplished by allowing a choice other than God. We have the opportunity to show our love for Him through our obedience to His commands. John 14:15 says, "If you love me, you will obey what I command." Through our obedience, we show God how very much we love Him.

God placed the choice of obedience or rebellion before Adam and Eve in the Garden of Eden, and He places the same choice before us every day. Not only does He give us the choice, but He also gives us the good and correct answer when we do make our choice. Yet, just like Adam and Eve so long ago, we often continue to choose the wrong answer no matter how clear God has made the correct response through His Word and the leading of the Spirit within us.

The Pop Quiz

Remember how it felt to walk into a classroom and have the professor announce a pop quiz? Whether you were prepared or unprepared, the unexpected announcement still brings a rush of anxiety. What if you don't know the answers? What if you forget?

As you sit with paper and pencil ready for the first question, the professor announces that he is also going to be giving you the answer to the questions. *Oh man, how could that be? What kind of pop quiz is this? Is he really going to provide both the question and the answer? This is even better than an open book quiz!* You start to relax, and although still a bit confused, you are ready when the first question is asked. "Are you supposed to eat of the tree of knowledge of good and evil?" And with only a very brief pause, the professor gives the class the answer:

"The correct answer to this question is no." Then he asks the second question: "What are the consequences of eating of that tree?" Again the correct answer immediately follows: "Death!"

As you sit there staring at your paper, you realize you have not written down either of the correct answers to the questions asked. Why not? What are you waiting for? Yes, he did present you with a test, but he's giving you the answers. You have the chance to make a perfect score on this one. What's the hesitation? You find yourself wondering what would happen if you gave a different answer. *After all, how important can this test really be if he's giving the answers? It probably won't really count in my final grade. This must just be a trial run, not the real thing. So why take it seriously if it's not for real? It's just a little thing. How big could the fallout really be?*

The longer you think about it, the more questioning thoughts start to fly through your mind:

- Maybe I didn't hear him right. Maybe it would be OK to eat of that tree.

- I'm a little confused as to which tree he said we weren't to eat from.

- It is called the tree of the Knowledge of Good and Evil. That sounds pretty good. Surely he wouldn't have said no to that tree.

- Anyone can make mistakes. Maybe he just gave the wrong answer.

- Since this is probably no big deal, I think I will try it my way.

- Maybe one little bite wouldn't matter.

Now think about this situation again. You are sitting in class and presented with a test. You are told you will be given the correct answers; all you have to do is write it down. Just how crazy would it be to write in a different answer than the one the professor has told you is the correct one? It would be nuts! But that's exactly what Adam and Eve did. Furthermore, each one of us has made this same decision at some point in our lives when we choose to give into temptation and sin. God gives us the right answer and the resources to succeed and yet we so often choose to fail the pop quiz.

The point of this analogy is that often we know the right answer, but we do the wrong thing anyway. Adam and Eve knew what was right, but they chose to do what was wrong. And we are just like them. We choose to rebel and live the exact way we know not to live. That being the case, we have to find the strength and the hope to make the right decision and do the right thing. We have to use the fellowship of others and the power of God if we are to stand up against temptations that are so appealing.

Satan's Tools

The substitutes that Satan offers may initially look similar to the spiritual fruit we know we need and have gone looking for. Let's consider the apple and tomato again. From a distance, these two look similar, and we may not be able to tell the difference. They are similar in color, size, and shape, and after all, they are both fruit. Satan knows that we are in search of the sweet taste and nourishment of the apple, but he lures us in by making what he has to offer look as much the same as he can, at least from a distance. What good would it do for him to know that we are searching for an apple and then try to offer us a cucumber? He knows that he wouldn't even get us to look twice at what he's proposing. He needs us to at least entertain the thought that what he's suggesting is close to what we are looking for if he's going to lure us away from God's blessings for us. So he makes what he has to offer look similar from a distance.

As a matter of fact, if we aren't discerning, Satan may even use things that we would determine to be "good" things for us to be involved in to draw us away. He not only uses things that are obviously sins no matter how you look at them, but he can also put "good" things in your path that can get you out of God's will for your life.

This is how he works. He doesn't get us to indulge in his substitutes by only offering rotten, sour-tasting fruit. No. He offers fruit that tastes, looks, and in all senses of the word is "good." But what happens if you get involved in something "good," but it is not what you are supposed to be doing? You are still standing outside of God's will for your life and are therefore sinning.

When I (Steve) weighed sixty pounds more than I do today, it was obviously not a good thing. Losing weight and getting my appetite for food under control would have been a very good thing. I had tried many things, but my appetite was ravenous. I had heard that a low-carbohydrate diet had helped many people lose weight very quickly. So I bought my carbohydrate-counting book, stuck it in my back pocket, and dug right into all the eggs, cheese, and meat I wanted. I did nothing about my appetite, but I did start losing weight. However, there were some other things that came along with the weight loss that were not so good.

First of all, I was hard to be with. I was very irritable and snippy at the least little thing. Not having carbohydrates had an unpleasant effect on my emotions. I was very uncomfortable with how I felt and how I interacted with others. Some of that mental irritation could have been a result of what was going on in my body. I was very uncomfortable because I was very constipated. It was serious business and produced serious pain.

Losing the weight brought out the worst in me. But I was so hooked on weight loss that I did not want to stop. So I did not, not until I had dropped about thirty pounds. That felt very good, and I felt great when people began to comment on my success. The weight loss looked and felt good, but it was not. It was a substitute for what was good.

What would have been good would have been bringing my appetite under control. The best thing would have been for me to have found a peace that would lessen my desire for food. I could have used my physical problem of too much weight to lead me to the solution of my spiritual and emotional problems behind the fat. I did not choose to do that. Instead, I ate and ate, amazed that I could still lose weight as long as I left off the breads, sweets, and vegetables I loved. My weight dropped, but my behavior did not change.

Living lighter was a freeing feeling, but I could not stay on the diet forever. I finally deprived myself long enough and returned to my normal eating routine. Within a short time I was back where I was with my weight but with a lot more frustration and a lot more fat than when I started. The quick weight loss had depleted me of muscle tissue, and I replaced that with fat. And I felt fatter. What had looked so good and felt so good in the beginning was not good at all. The fast weight-loss plan prevented me from finding what would have been truly good for me.

As we battle our various appetites, some choices look like the good and right thing to do but may not be what God is asking us to do. If it's not God's plan for you, then you could be following Satan's substitutes and allowing him to pull you away from what God has in store for you. You may want to evaluate yourself and your activities and see who you are following. Are you relying on your self-effort and sense of independence? Are you refusing to ask for help from your spiritual brothers and sisters because you need to look strong? Have you agreed to teach a Sunday school class just because your pastor asked you to instead of asking God if that was how He wanted you to serve Him? Are you helping others to the extent that you are neglecting yourself or your family? Are you serving God with the wrong motives? Any of these can be substitutes that Satan is offering you. They look good on the surface, but their ultimate purpose is to draw you away from God and into disobedience.

Satan's subtlety in offering substitutes that look good from a distance is how he so easily ensnares us. Once we have given Satan's proposition a second glance, he begins the art of deceiving us into believing that what we are looking at really is what we need. It's appealing to the eye, at least from a distance. But as we get closer to Satan's substitute, we begin to notice the difference. However, by now we have been listening to Satan's deceptions long enough that he has us convinced that his substitute will be "close enough" to satisfy. By the time we reach the fruit, we are so deceived that we can make ourselves believe that Satan's fruit really is just what we have been searching for. It's not until we take a great big bite out of the fruit that Satan offers that we realize that the taste in our mouth is not at all what we expected. How very wrong we were! And even then, sometimes we may convince ourselves to continue eating Satan's fruit because we believe it's all we have. We may not even notice the genuine fruit right beside us.

The fruit of the Spirit is always available to us as Christians, but Satan is the master deceiver and works to convince us that it is not and that we must settle for substitutes. We may say to ourselves, "I have no willpower, no self-control," and just give into our temptations. But the Bible tells us that self-control is a fruit of the Spirit that is available to help us overcome temptation.

WHAT ARE YOU FILLING UP ON?

Are we making the best and healthiest choices? Or are we just settling for what's easiest, quickest, or most pleasing at the moment?

Raising my daughter Madeline has been one of the greatest joys in my (Steve's) life. Establishing boundaries for her concerning food and other things has been hard, but that is what she has needed me to do as a father. Madeline has a ravenous appetite. She loves good food, and I love to give it to her. At the dinner table she will eat the best of nutritious food and love it. But I have to limit what she eats before the meal. Any good parent does that. If Madeline eats before dinner, she won't eat a nutritious meal.

I am the one who sets the limits at a time when Madeline is not mature enough to do so. The more I do it, the more structure she internalizes and the easier it becomes for her to delay gratification and wait for dinner and the delicious, healthy food that awaits her. All of us need to do the same. The same is true for us: We need to say no to some forbidden fruit before dinner so we can enjoy God's fruit that is spiritually fulfilling.

When we are growing spiritually, the fruit of the Spirit is very appealing to us. We believe that only this fruit will truly fill our appetite. When we are filled up with the fruit of the Spirit, we have much less desire to be filled with forbidden fruits. However, when we are not filling our appetite for fruit with what the Spirit has to offer, we still have an appetite, and forbidden fruit begins to look more and more appealing. When we fill ourselves up with forbidden fruit, we will experience less desire for the fruit of the Spirit.

TEMPTATION

Scripture tells us, "No temptation has seized you except what is common to man. And God is faithful; he will not let you be tempted beyond what you can bear. But when you are tempted, he will also provide a way out so that you can stand up under it" (1 Corinthians 10:13).

Temptation is a part of life on this earth. We have all experienced temptation and will continue to experience it until our dying breath; so we had better figure out what we are going to do to fight against it and respond to it with the "right" answer. An important note to point out here is that being tempted is not a sin. Even Jesus was tempted, yet He never sinned. So it's not the temptation crossing our path that makes us sinners; it is how we respond to that temptation that is the determining factor.

Satan's job is to tempt us. Our job is to stand firm against these temptations and to resist him. Satan may place a thought in our minds or a sight in our line of vision as a temptation. If we choose to dwell on that thought or vision, then we have sinned.

Satan doesn't tempt us where we have no appetite. What good would it do for him to tempt us in an area that we have no desire? None. Instead, he hits us where we already experience some desire, want, or appetite. Then he grows that temptation bigger, bit by bit. He starts with little thoughts at first that we allow ourselves to entertain as "innocent." And before long, the desire has grown so big within us that all Satan has to do is stand back and give a little nudge to cause us to completely crumble. He may have convinced us that we are being deprived of some essential element or activity that we deserve to have. When this happens, watch out!

Remember that although Satan is a spiritual being, he has no authority in the spiritual world. The battle over who would control our spirits was fought long ago, and Satan lost. So the battle for your spirit is over. Once you accept Jesus Christ as your Savior, there is nothing Satan can do about it.

THE TEMPTATION OF JESUS

In the desert, Satan tempted Jesus in the areas of human appetite. Jesus's desire was strong in these areas; had He been like most of us, He very easily could have fallen into Satan's traps. When the Bible says, "No temptation has seized you except what is common to man" (1 Corinthians 10:13), we can be assured that Jesus was tempted at the same level and in some of the same areas in which we are tempted. Satan did not just place some little, easy to ignore temptations before the Son of God. He went for the jugular! He knew Jesus well, and he placed before Him three temptations that he knew would be almost impossible to resist. Let's look at each of the human appetites Satan used to tempt the Son of God.

First, Satan hit Jesus with the appetite for food. "After fasting forty days and forty nights, he [Jesus] was hungry. The tempter came to him and said, 'If you are the Son of God, tell these stones to become bread'" (Matthew 4:2–3). Have you ever fasted for forty days and nights? Can you imagine just how deprived and hungry Jesus must have felt by the time Satan showed up?

When Satan came to tempt Jesus, he knew exactly where to hit that would strike the hardest blow possible. Satan knew that Jesus had been fasting and immediately tempted Him with food. Because Jesus was totally man and totally God, He had the same physical needs and desires that we have. Any human body that has gone without food for forty days and nights is going to experience an extremely strong craving for food. But instead of giving into His physical needs, Jesus held His spiritual needs of pleasing God as more important.

Second, Satan presented Jesus with a temptation regarding the appetite for prestige. "And then the devil took him to the holy city and had him stand on the highest point of the temple. 'If you are the Son of God,' he said, 'throw yourself down. For it is written: "He will command his angels concerning you, and they will lift you up in their hands, so that you will not strike your foot against a stone"'" (Matthew 4:5–6). We all want to be a "somebody," and how better to prove that you are a "somebody" than to have ten thousand angels come soaring in to rescue you?

We can only imagine how very much Jesus wanted to prove to his archenemy and the rest of the world that He was who He said He was. Jesus knew that He was the King of kings and Lord of lords. He was the Creator of all things and the Redeemer of the world. If that were true of us, we would have wanted to toot our own horn, to stand up and shout to the world, "Look at me! See who I am. Worship me!" But that was not to be a part of God's plan and was therefore a temptation that Jesus had to resist, which He did without denying who He is.

Finally, Satan tempted Jesus with two of the most powerful human appetites: power and possessions. "Again, the devil took him to a very high mountain and showed him all the kingdoms of the world and their splendor. 'All this I will give you,' he said, 'if you will bow down and worship me'" (Matthew 4:8–9). By offering Jesus all the kingdoms of the world, Satan was presenting Jesus with the opportunity to exert His power and authority here on earth. This had to be a pleasing thought, at least to the human side of Jesus. Jesus knew that most of the people of earth did not understand who He really was. How easy it would have been to say to Himself, "If I could have power and authority over all these kingdoms, then these people whom I love so much would have the proof they need to believe in Me. I could have so much more influence from that vantage point."

How often do we take a suggestion from Satan and decide that it makes more sense to do it that way than the way God already lined up? We decide to help God out just a little—after all, "He probably didn't think of doing it this way." That might sound ridiculous to some of you, but you can probably remember similar thoughts going through your head on more than one occasion. It is so easy to keep looking for something that seems like a better way than the one God clearly outlined for us. Jesus had to resist the temptation of what looked good and to remember that God's plan is the only way to go.

During this temptation, Satan presented Jesus with not only the opportunity for earthly power and authority, but also for possessions. This is an area where many of us have a very soft spot. Satan offered Jesus not only the kingdoms of the world, but also "their splendor." That means all the wealth, beautiful homes, best cars, newest and neatest gadgets, and much more were at Jesus's fingertips. Remember, Jesus was human and had the desires that humans have, one of which is often the desire to acquire. Here Satan is presenting a poor carpenter with winning the lottery. He would have more money and possessions than he could ever use. Think how easy it would have been for Jesus to rationalize how He would be sure to tithe His 10 percent (and maybe a little more for good measure) and that He would share His wealth with the underprivileged. Jesus could have convinced Himself that He would use the money to go about doing the will of God. But Jesus knew that was not the will of God, and He therefore resisted the temptation and commanded Satan to leave His presence.

When you look at these temptations, you can't help but notice a glaring fault in Satan's strategy—a fault that shows how we, too, can have victory over the temptations that confront us. Satan tempted Jesus with things he already had. Everything Satan held in front of Jesus as something to have or experience were items that Jesus could have or experience on His own. If Jesus had wanted to ride around Jerusalem in a 2033 Cadillac, He could have. To Him, the universe was unrestricted by time or space. There was nothing Satan could offer Jesus that He could not offer Himself. All that Satan's temptations did was try to get Jesus to experience these things off schedule, at a time that would not honor God.

So it is with us. God will give us the desires of our hearts—but not right now. Not in this moment when we demand them, and not in the form we think they should come in. God will not fulfill us or meet our appetite needs in an instant, but He will satisfy us. If we get off His timetable by impulsively gratifying our desires, then we will never experience God meeting our need and providing abundance in our lives. We won't ever know satisfaction or the peace that is beyond all understanding. Today, Satan will tempt you with things that are already available to you in Christ. But Satan will tempt you to look to him for satisfaction, and when you do he will destroy you with the very things God intends for you to have in His timing. You may have picked up this book because you are tired of Satan doing that to you at every turn. When temptation comes, don't think about having to have satisfaction now. Think about the honor of God giving you the desires of your heart in His own time.

SURRENDER

Before we surrender to God, we are doing everything under our own power. The power that could not prevent the problem is not going to be the power that will fix it. You don't have it in you—your sinful nature and sick mind—to find answers that will fix the problem. Your life has most likely already proven that what you have within you and the remedies you have attempted are not enough to satisfy your appetites and do battle to regain freedom. Your only hope is to find victory by surrendering your life to God. Admit to God that the problem grew out of control under your own power. Believe that God cares about you and will fill you with His power and change your life through that power. Then allow God to do it.

Surrender means you no longer try to face the problem alone. With God and fellow strugglers, you empower yourself to go a single day without responding to your appetite. Or maybe one day is too long. Perhaps you have to take life one hour at a time, surrendering more and more of yourself to God's control. Agree to be less agitated with what is out of your control, and be courageous to work hard with what is in your control. Surrender is the beginning to healing.

Surrender to God is giving up and giving in, not to defeat, but to a new way of living that can lead to the satisfaction of all your appetites. It also brings your life back under control. God cannot fight this battle for you. He will stand beside you, providing you with all you need to

FOOD FOR THOUGHT

Sometimes it helps to see exactly what a choice entails. We encourage each of you to use the following list to evaluate your own situation with regard to spiritual appetite. Take a moment to study these two lists. Does the fruit of your life demonstrate your most important commitment?

Characteristics of Forbidden Fruit	Characteristics of the Spirit
Interested in pleasing self	Interested in pleasing God
Seeks pleasure to avoid pain	Seeks God to avoid death
Focused on the temporal	Focused on the eternal
Trusts in Satan's lies	Trusts in God's truth
Enslaved	Free
Worships self, idols, gods	Worships God alone
Thinks about sinful things	Thinks about what pleases the Spirit
Fights urges alone	Fights urges with the Spirit's help
Seeks immediate gratification	Delays gratification
Lacks self-control	Exhibits self-control
Governed by the five senses	Governed by Scripture
Relies on self	Relies on the Holy Spirit

win hands down. But it is up to you to use what He offers and to fight the fight.

Respond in the Spirit

The Bible offers at least two good illustrations of how we can respond to trials. Three different approaches can lead people to respond to the world around them in very different ways.[2] As we look at these examples, consider where you would be. Which self would have controlled your decisions and actions? First, let's consider the story of the good Samaritan from Luke 10:30–37.

As you may recall, a man traveled down the road to Jericho and was met by some men who attacked, robbed, and left him for dead at the side of the road. Before long, a priest and then later a Levite were traveling down the road. When they each saw the hurt man, they moved to the other side of the road to pass by. Finally, a Samaritan man, traveling down the same road, saw the injured man and stopped to help him.

As we study this parable, we can easily see who was following which part of themselves. The robbers obviously made their decisions based on fleshly and self-gratifying selves. They were only concerned about meeting their own needs. The priest and the Levite allowed their rationalizing self to be in control. They probably altered reality in their minds by telling themselves something like, "If I walk on the other side of the road I can convince myself, or at least pretend, that I never saw the man." They were men of high standing, and it just would not have been proper for them to soil themselves by helping this man. "What would people think?" Then there was the Samaritan man, who allowed his Spirit-controlled self to be in charge of his decisions. He knew that the Jews and Samaritans were practically enemies and that people may think less of him if he stopped to help this man. But the injured man needed help, and that was what was most important. Doing what God would have him do, regardless of the consequences, was what motivated the good Samaritan to offer help to a stranger in need.

As we begin to fight the battle with our appetites, we will soon see that we have three choices available to us as to how we respond to temptation. First, we can respond through our fleshly self that focuses on fulfilling our fleshly desires through immediate gratification and impulsiveness. Our fleshly self is driven to act out of simple reflex and is focused on self-fulfillment and pleasure. Second, we can respond to the temptation through our rationalizing or intellectual self, which provides excuses and explanations that may alter reality in our minds in order to make our choice more acceptable to us. Our rationalizing self is more concerned with the reactions of others and the personal consequences we may experience as a result of our choices. Finally, we can respond through our Spirit-controlled self, which involves seeking God's solution to the problem or temptation and doing what He would have us do. Our Spirit-controlled self seeks God's will regardless of the consequences.

Let's consider one more example, recorded in John chapters 18 and 19, which describe the trial of Jesus. In summary, Jesus had been betrayed by Judas, arrested by soldiers, and brought before the high priest. He was then presented before Pilate, where the crowd, officials, and high priest shouted accusations about Jesus and demanded that He be crucified. Pilate talked with Jesus and attempted to reason with the crowd since he found no guilt in Jesus. But the anger of the crowd continued to escalate while Pilate continued to look for a way around this uncomfortable situation. Finally, Pilate handed Jesus over to be crucified. All the while, Jesus did as His Father requested: He surrendered His will to the will of the Father, even to the point of death.

In this illustration, as in the first, the various responses are easily identified. The crowd, soldiers, high priest, and Judas all followed their fleshly selves. They were interested only in what they wanted and they did what they had to do to get it *now!* There was no putting them off, delaying their desire, or reasoning with them. Pilate, on the other hand, responded through his rationalizing self. He tried on more than one occasion to get Jesus to give him a reason not to crucify Him, which He never did. Pilate also tried to reason with the crowd and even offered them a substitute to hopefully fulfill their fleshly desire for blood, but they would have nothing of it. He came at this conflict from several different intellectual angles, but all to no avail.

Finally, there is Jesus. He is our best example. He followed His Spirit-controlled self and did what God was asking Him to do, no matter what the consequences were. Jesus so wanted to be obedient to God that He was even willing to die if necessary—and it was.

If you are going to be victorious over your appetites, you must not respond to impulse as your fleshly self would have you do. And you must stop attempting to alter reality through excuses or explanations as your rationalizing self would have you do. You must learn to live under the Holy Spirit's control, doing first and foremost what God would have you to do.

What are these tools, these techniques of suffering, these means of experiencing the pain of problems constructively that I call discipline? There are four: delaying of gratification, acceptance of responsibility, dedication to truth, and balancing . . . they are simple tools, and almost all children are adept in their use by the age of ten. Yet presidents and kings will often forget to use them, to their downfall.

—M. SCOTT PECK, *THE ROAD LESS TRAVELED*

8

NEW PATHWAYS

L EARNING TO BRING YOUR APPETITES and therefore your life under control requires that you begin to understand the concepts of balance and moderation. The Bible tells us that "The man who fears God will avoid all extremes" (Ecclesiastes 7:18).

Consider what life looks like without moderation. Have you ever tried to balance on a teeter-totter? If you have, you soon realized that you cannot balance by standing on either end of the board. Only as you only begin to move up the board toward the center point will you be successful. The closer you get to the middle, the closer you are to balance. But once you get to the center, if you just keep walking toward the other end, you quickly become off-balance again.

Life is like a teeter-totter with moderation being the pivotal point of balance. Standing, or living, at either extreme does not produce a sense of balance in your life. So in regard to life, what exactly is at each of the two ends of the teeter-totter? At one end is excessive indulgence, and at the other is total restriction. Living in either excessive indulgence or total restriction of our God-given appetites, which by nature are healthy and appropriate, will lead us to a life that is out of balance.

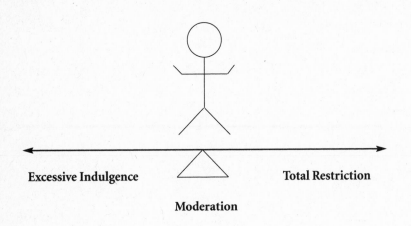

Excessive Indulgence   **Total Restriction**

Moderation

TOTAL RESTRICTION

There are elements in our lives that we do need to *totally restrict* ourselves from. Such desires have been distorted by our sinful natures and are destructive or inappropriate for us to engage in at *any* level—desires for things or activities such as pornography, illicit sex, and illegal drugs.

Let's look at what a life focused on total restriction of our healthy appetites looks like. We have all at one time or another attempted to restrict ourselves from some substance or activity, the most common being food. Judging from rising statistics, it appears we aren't restricting our food intake as much as we might think.[1] But because so many people are overweight, you can find people all around you on any given day in some stage of food restriction. They may be restricting themselves from high-fat, high-calorie foods, sugars, or carbohydrates. But if these diet plans are taken to the extreme of total restriction, they can have some negative consequences. Our bodies need a combination of vitamins and minerals that come from a wide variety of foods. Totally restricting your consumption of a particular food group can cause your body to become depleted of its needed nutrients and result in physical damage.

Another negative consequence to total restriction of any natural appetite, including food, is the development of a sense of deprivation that may lead to stronger cravings for the desired substance. We become emotionally and spiritually weakened, and Satan has a foothold through which to tempt us. If the total restriction continues, it is more likely that a person will eventually not only indulge in the desired substance but binge on it. Therefore, it is through our attempt to totally control and restrict our appetites that our appetites actually grow to the point of being out of control. By the time we give in to them, they have become hungry beasts that require more and more to satiate.

The cycle becomes automatic. We seek control over our appetites, which leads to the extreme conditions of total restriction. As this continues, our appetites grow and begin to scream to be filled. We are only capable of resisting their demands for so long. Eventually we give in to the point of excessive indulgence. It is this sense of failure to control our desires that leads to feelings of guilt. In our mind, we determine to once again gain control over our appetites. And the cycle begins again, only this time the hole needing to be filled will be a little deeper as a result of the hurt, pain, and lowered self-esteem of the past failure. As the cycle plays out, it will take more and more of the substance desired to attempt to fill the void. This is how appetites that were once good can so easily turn destructive.

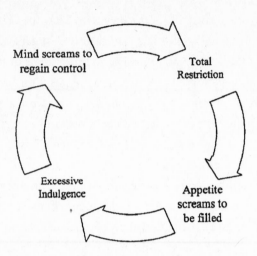

Although this is the cycle that most people will tend to fall into when they attempt to totally restrict themselves, there is that small percentage of the population who will even take restriction to its extreme. A person struggling with an appetite for food who takes restriction to this end will eventually suffer from anorexia, which occurs when a person stops eating almost all food. If this behavior continues, starvation is imminent. The disease can lead to death if not treated.

Granted, there are some things that fall into this "total-restriction" category for certain people but not for others, such as alcohol and certain foods. A person may need to classify a food or activity in the total-restriction group due to health problems, addiction, or family history. But in general, our God-given desires were intended to bring us pleasure and to be experienced in moderation rather than eliminated entirely.

EXCESSIVE INDULGENCE

At the other end of the teeter-totter is *excessive indulgence*. This concept is not hard to conceive of if you live in the United States. Excess is defined as an "action that goes beyond a reasonable limit. An amount greater than is necessary."[2] Our motto in America seems to be "the more, the better"—no matter what it's more of. Just look at some of these statistics:

- Obesity rates have reached an all-time high of more than 30 percent of adults.[3]

- One out of five Americans has a sexually transmitted disease.[4]

- Television viewing has now reached 3 to 5 hours per day, depending on age.[5]

- Addictions now affect an astonishing 30 percent of American families.[6]

- Personal bankruptcies filed in 2001 numbered 1,452,030.[7]

- The average household has 16.7 credit cards with credit-card balances averaging almost $9,000 per household.[8]

- Consumer credit has reached an all-time high of over 19 percent of personal income.[9]

- There are now more registered cars on the road than there are licensed drivers.[10]

The problem isn't the enjoyment of pleasure through indulging; it is when our seeking of pleasure is unrestrained to the point that we forget all else and are no longer concerned about the consequences—at least not at the moment. This is when we become totally self-focused and have begun to worship an idol. This is excessive indulgence.

A life of excessive indulgence is a life full of sin. God speaks often about partaking in activities around us according to His set of rules and with moderation and self-control. He even talks about our need to restrict our behaviors in certain areas—either when they are in opposition to His commandments or when partaking may cause a spiritual brother to stumble (1 Corinthians 8; 10:23–32; Galatians 5:16–21). Nowhere in Scripture does God give us permission to indulge excessively in the things of this world. There is no activity, substance, or desire on this earth that cannot become sinful when engaged in to excess. Reason is no longer in control; therefore, our desire to consume controls us.

More and more people who have problems with spending are showing up in counseling offices and calling *New Life Live.* Their buying has spun out of control. In some cases, the spending can become so severe that it is life threatening or, more likely, threatening a significant relationship or marriage. Here are some very serious examples.

- A middle-aged married woman has repeatedly racked up tens of thousands of dollars in credit-card debt mainly by watching the various home-shopping channels. She is lonely and depressed and is trying to use things to fill the void she feels. She reports feeling driven to buy more and more, even though once she gets it she has to hide it in her closet so her husband won't know. Her marriage is teetering, along with her sense of self-worth after her husband made the inevitable discovery.

- A single lady in her midforties is living on welfare and food stamps. She is so limited in available money and resources that she experiences a chronic sense of deprivation in her life. Although her budget indicates that she is capable of covering her expenses, each month her bank statement shows the account is significantly overdrawn. She reports an inability to control her impulsive and compulsive shopping and has now had her bank account closed. She is in danger of being evicted from her home if she cannot stop indulging.

The main problem with living a life at either extreme is that you may actually find yourself jumping back and forth between them as a feeble attempt to regain balance. Regardless of whether you enter the cycle at one end (total restriction) or the other (excessive indulgence), the cycle is still the same and will become increasingly destructive if not stopped.

Seek Balance

We are free to do whatever it is that we desire, whether to indulge or to deprive. This is the case for all humans because of free will. Scripture speaks directly to these issues of freedom in Christ: "But food does not bring us near to God; we are no worse if we do not eat, and no better if we do" (1 Corinthians 8:4, 8).

Our brain wants to restore balance internally for our physical and emotional well-being. When you experience an intense emotion such as anger, anxiety, or sadness, your brain signals your body to start searching for a way to restore balance. It will begin looking for things that you have trained it to look for based on past experiences. Your brain remembers that a particular activity brought on a chemical change that can restore balance. If the behavior that brings momentary balance is actually unhealthy, we must find new pathways to lead us into balance.

Distinguish Between Wants and Needs

We live in a society that has compounded the confusion between what we truly need and the things we merely want. We are bombarded every day with advertising that tries to convince us that we need a new car, whiter teeth, a different hair color, the newest electronic gadget, or the magic cure to lose weight. Commercials and billboards and ads in magazines rarely advertise something we really do need.

Companies try to convince us that something we want is really something we desperately need. If we see and hear this enough, we just might start to believe it. (That's what the advertisers are banking on.) Our society feeds on, and in some cases even creates, our desires. Over time as we continue to entertain these desires, they grow stronger and stronger. Eventually we may convince ourselves that we *need* them.

If this becomes the case, we focus more and more on the supposed need, which drives our appetite into high gear and pulls all our focus to the desire to fill the appetite. As the desire becomes stronger, it becomes even harder to deny our appetite. We may even reach a point of rationalizing to ourselves that our "needs" are just different than most other people's. Rationalization is a great defense mechanism that helps us get what we want without having to feel guilty about it.

One question remains: how do we go about practically managing the appetites we will inevitably encounter? This list of skills and suggestions has been collected from a variety of sources, with a few additions of our own.[11]

Practice Moderation. Moderation is, of course, the *best* strategy for learning to control your appetites instead of your appetites controlling you. Learning to seek moderation instead of excessive indulgence or total restriction for nondestructive appetites is how you reach a sense of balance. In truth, moderately indulging in your appetite before it grows too strong will help you avoid overindulging. For example, you may want to allow yourself to watch one hour of television and then turn it off instead of sitting in front of it all evening. Or consider how you would be much better off to eat before you are ravenous, because if you deprive yourself to that point, you are very likely going to binge.

Appropriate desires are satisfied with the actual desired substance or activity. Substitutions often will not adequately satisfy. So if it's not destructive to you or others, consider how to best satisfy that desire in moderation. For example, if you really want ice cream, substituting celery sticks will not likely satisfy that craving. So consider allowing yourself some ice cream, but don't eat the entire half-gallon.

Over the years there have been many studies on what are the keys to keeping weight off. There really is not one particular diet that brings the appetite under control, nor is there a plan that works for most people. But when you look at the small percentage who actually do keep the weight off, you find one skill that they have in common. It is not going the longest without the most food or anything similar. They simply have developed the ability to consistently restrain their eating. Those who are successful in weight loss have come to a different place emotionally and spiritually. They need less from food because they receive more satisfaction from God and friends. As a result, they have learned to eat smaller portions and cut off potential binges by becoming satisfied with less. What works with food will work in other areas. But the big dilemma is how difficult it is to do it.

Use Self-Talk. We all talk to ourselves whether we want to admit it or not. Learning to use your self-talk to your benefit can greatly improve your success in fighting your appetites. Learn to fight back against the cravings. This involves using your anger to your advantage. Get mad at the craving, especially if it's an unhealthy or inappropriate desire. Instead of getting mad at yourself for experiencing or giving into the craving, get mad before you indulge. Direct your anger to the source instead of at yourself. Confront yourself and your appetites if necessary in order to bring rationality back into play. When we actively engage our minds in talking to ourselves, we are less likely to fall into the trap of acting without thinking. Not only are we thinking when we are using self-talk, we are also determining what it is we want to believe.

You can also use self-talk to reward yourself for successfully controlling an appetite that threatened to gain control. Give yourself a pat on the back for a job well done, and file these successes away in memory for use as encouragement and support during future battles.

Start Thought Stopping. Thought stopping is the process of learning to take control of what you are thinking. Regardless of whether we are paying any attention, our brain is always thinking about something. You may have noticed this on those occasions where you seem to get a song stuck in your head. Even when you aren't consciously thinking about much of anything, there comes that song again. You may even shake it off and go on about your business, only to be bombarded with the song over and over.

Your mind is always thinking. It doesn't like to go completely quiet and will therefore go in search of past thoughts to fill any dead space. That's how the song keeps showing up. When your mind goes blank, it will immediately return to the last most-prominent thought to pull back up. When you have been actively battling a particular appetite, the last most prominent thought very likely will be something about that appetite. It is through this process that we begin to feel tortured and run down by the very appetite we are trying to control. The appetite eventually seems to "get the best of us" and we give in.

Thought stopping begins as soon as you become consciously aware of what you are thinking about (you can't do anything to control the thoughts you are having at a subconscious level). As soon as you identify a thought as something negative or detrimental for you to be thinking about, you simply say "stop" to yourself in your mind or out loud (2 Corinthians 10:5). Be firm and strong. You are taking control of your thinking; this is no time to be a wimp. The key to this process is what happens next. If you simply say "stop" and then go about whatever you were doing, your mind will go blank again, and the thought about your appetite will return.

After you have taken control and commanded an unhealthy thought to stop, you must then choose what you are going to think about next. If you don't replace the unhealthy thought with something healthier, you may as well not have even tried to stop the original thought in the first place. You can replace the negative thought with anything positive; a memory verse, your favorite praise and worship chorus, a pleasant childhood memory, plans for your next vacation . . . anything that you enjoy.

The pattern of having a negative thought, telling it to stop, and replacing it with a positive thought is a cycle you will likely repeat over and over as you start to retrain your thought patterns. However, the good news is that eventually you will have replaced a negative thought with a positive one so many times that the next time your brain goes blank and starts searching for the last most prominent thought, it will come up with the positive thoughts you have been using. When that happens, you will have retrained your mind to think differently.

Raise Your Body Temperature. This may be one of the simplest of all the suggestions, but it has been shown to work. It's true that merely increasing your body temperature can satisfy many cravings. So get out there and do some moving around. Your body temperature increases as your activity increases. You may want to try some light exercise like stretching, calisthenics, going up and down some steps or walking around the block. Anything you can do that will get your blood pumping just a little harder can help you not just ignore but actually satisfy your craving.

Pamper Yourself. This is part of training your brain to gain a sense of pleasure from new and different activities. Your brain learns and remembers activities that bring pleasure in order to drive you toward those activities during times of stress. It uses the pleasure derived from these specific activities to regain a sense of balance internally. If the activity you have been engaging in for pleasure is something that you now wish to manage or control, what better way to do so than with something else you enjoy? To do this, you can use anything that brings you a sense of pleasure and that is not harmful to you or those around you.

Distract or Delay the Decision. This tactic relies on the fact that most appetites last only for a few minutes. So, if you can, delay your decision to act on the desire you are having for fifteen to thirty minutes and then see if you really still want it. Be sure to use distraction and diversion during the delay, or you may just find yourself watching the clock and thinking about how much longer until you get to indulge. If you get involved in something else and after the thirty minutes you still want whatever it is that you desired, go ahead and enjoy it, in moderation. Sometimes we just can't outwait our appetites, so as long as they are not destructive, this is one of those times where indulging with moderation is the right thing to do.

Engage in Self-Monitoring. Controlling our appetites has everything to do with getting to know ourselves better. Ask yourself what you are feeling before you indulge in a craving. Cravings often mask some negative emotion that you would just as soon not experience. This may be anger, depression, anxiety, boredom, loneliness, or any host of other emotions. Once you have identified the feeling behind the drive, you can more appropriately express or deal with your feelings, instead of simply trying to ignore it by engaging in some appetite that you believe will make the negative feeling disappear. When you learn to express your feeling appropriately, your appetites can stop being emotional buffers and once again serve the purposes God intended them to serve.

Fellowship with God. When you have an appetite that needs to be fed, you have a choice as to how you are going to feed it. Almost all our appetites have in common their focus on feeding the flesh. However, we have another choice: we can choose to feed our spirit and strengthen ourselves from the inside out. As we spend time with our heavenly Father, we will be gaining wisdom and understanding, as well as growing stronger spiritually and thus more able to utilize the resources He makes available to us. Through this growth, we will better understand and use the weapons He gives us to fight the good fight and to stand firm against temptation.

Of all these suggestions, this last option is by far the most effective. As we fellowship with God through time spent in His Word, with fellow believers, and while serving others, we open ourselves to a lasting fulfillment that may satisfy better than any other craving or desire we might choose instead. We have instant accountability, structure, and support when we surround ourselves with His church. Contemplate this thought as we turn to the next chapter and discover how to cultivate a divine appetite.

HEALTHY ALTERNATIVES FOR THE UNHEALTHY APPETITE

Each of these alternative activities is a healthy means of filling our natural desires by building us up, bringing us pleasure, and satisfying our desires. None will cause you to feel guilty or require you to seek forgiveness after participating in them.[12] By engaging in activities you find enjoyable, you will give your brain a whole new set of pleasurable activities to call on in times of stress. Just remember that moderation is the goal in all activities. You're not trying to replace the obsession or excessive indulgence with another activity.

1. Get some exercise. This is probably the healthiest alternative imaginable. Not only is exercise the number-one stress reducer, it also controls appetite, increases energy and body temperature, releases endorphins, and improves sleep quality. Physical exercise is the most natural way you can come to experience a state of well-being or satisfaction.

2. Listen to music. Music has been shown to cause a variety of emotional states in those listening. When you need to relax, listen to some calming music. If you need some extra energy, find something upbeat that makes you want to move. Be aware of your moods and your needs, and you will find that music can play a big part in helping you achieve a positive emotional state.

3. Get a massage. Not only is massage a wonderful way to pamper yourself, it also has several positive benefits. Massage creates a feeling of relaxation and peace, decreases stress and anxiety, and it reduces blood pressure. Getting a massage also helps improve your self-esteem because you are acknowledging that you *deserve* to be pampered. And a final benefit of massage is that it helps to fulfill our basic human need for caring touch.

4. Take a bath. Go the extra mile and make it a bubble bath or use some aromatherapy. A warm, soothing bath will produce feelings of relaxation and pleasure.

5. Read. Taking time to read a good book, an inspirational story from a magazine, or even the comics or sports page of the newspaper. What you enjoy will be unique to you, so don't get stuck in the rut of comparing yourself to others. Just find what type of reading material brings you pleasure and start reading it as often as you can.

6. Get some R&R. Learn more fun ways to rest and relax, and do it more often. There may be some things that you can do on a daily or weekly basis that will help you put the stresses of the world behind you.

But we believe it is also important to have more significant getaways that last for a couple of days or more. Vacation time really does make a difference in your mind-set and outlook. How long has it been since you really got away for some serious R&R?

7. Pray and meditate on Scripture. Through our personal time of prayer and meditation on God's Word, we will find the "peace that passes understanding." Spending time in God's presence helps us remember who we are and how very much we are loved. Talk about putting a smile on your face! Scripture tells us Jesus often went to a place by Himself and prayed (Matthew 14:23, 26:36–44; Mark 1:35, 6:46; Luke 5:16, 9:28–29; John 17).

Scripture tells us we should pray continuously (1 Thessalonians 5:17; Ephesians 6:18), we should be devoted to prayer (Colossians 4:2), we should pray to help us avoid temptation (Luke 22:40), and when we don't know what to say, the Spirit will intercede for us (Romans 8:26–27). We are also instructed to bring everything to God in prayer (Philippians 4:6) and to pray when in trouble (James 5:13).

8. Talk to a friend or therapist. Not only does talking through your stresses with a close confidant help relieve those stresses, but it will also help you feel more connected to another human being.

9. Keep a journal. Spend some time alone, just to consult your thoughts and feelings. Then take some time to journal about what's going on in your life and how you feel about things. Journaling can help you sort out the many things that may be going on in your head and heart. Once you have expressed your feelings in writing, they become much easier to understand and control.

10. Learn deep breathing and relaxation skills. Learning to relax through the use of deep breathing and relaxation skills will serve as a great way to reduce your tension and stress. If you want deep breathing to work, however, you must use your diaphragm in the same manner that professional singers do. When you breathe this way you will find that it is your stomach that moves, not your chest. This is our most natural form of breathing. When you watch newborn babies breathe, you see their little stomachs are going in and out—not their chests. This is the way we were created to breathe. But somewhere along the way we have been told to "suck in that stomach and stick out that chest," and we have moved away from our natural breathing. It is this diaphragmatic breathing that will instill a sense of relaxation internally. Why not start practicing today?

11. Become involved in discipleship. Discipleship involves growing in wisdom and knowledge of God through the process of gathering together with other believers. This involves more than just your personal quiet time. It is the fellowship of believers that results in building each other up, mentoring and accountability, and Bible study. Discipleship serves the purpose of spiritual growth and gives us a sense of connection and belonging that we all need.

12. Do something for someone else. The process of giving to and doing for others can lift your spirit and bring about a sense of pleasure faster than just about anything else. When you give of yourself altruistically, you are focusing on what you can do for someone else. You have moved away from a focus on self to a focus on others, and this is always a good place to be. There is an additional byproduct of altruism beyond the great feeling you will have for giving to those around you. You will likely notice that as you give, you begin to realize that you are useful and have something to offer to others. You begin to feel more valuable—thus enhancing your own self-esteem as well.

13. Laugh. Laughter is good medicine, especially when it comes to managing stress and increasing pleasure in life. Laughter is the natural expression of pleasure and fun. The more we can include laughter in our lives, the better we will feel physically and emotionally.

14. Find a hobby. If you don't already have a hobby, find one. If you do have one, start doing it actively. Make the time to do some of the things you enjoy on a regular basis. So often we allow ourselves to get so busy with the ins and outs of our daily life that we put our hobbies on the back burner or maybe forget about them altogether. Hobbies bring us pleasure, and if we are going to be successful in overcoming our appetites, we could use all the sources of pleasure we can find. So pull out those old golf clubs, clean up the paintbrushes, find the knitting needles, or untangle the fishing poles, and head for some fun.

15. Attend a meeting. Rather than get on the Internet to view pornography or charge up your credit cards with items you don't need or place a bet you probably won't win, get up and go to a meeting. Call a church and find out when their Christian recovery or support groups are meeting. Call information and get the number for Alcoholics Anonymous. Find out when and where the next meeting is happening near you. You will be surprised at what going to a meeting will do for you.

Meeting others who are struggling and hearing how God is working in their lives will help you believe He is also working in your life. At least that's what meetings do for me (Steve). I was at a very low point in my life when a friend took me to a twelve-step meeting. We sat there and I said nothing. There was nothing sensational or dynamic about the meeting, but every person who spoke talked of a fear-based life. I realized by listening that I had a lot in common with these people. Then they shared how God was working in their lives, and I came to believe He must be doing the same in the midst of my despair.

You don't have to be a member of a group to benefit. You can do what I did and just go to observe. But by the time the meeting is over, there is a very good chance you will see your life improve.

But seek first his kingdom and his righteousness,
and all these things will be given to you as well.

—MATTHEW 6:33

9

CULTIVATING
A DIVINE APPETITE

G OD IS THE KEY TO ANY SUCCESS you may have in learning to control your appetites. He needs to be your energy source, your pilot, and most of all, your foundation if you want to become a new creature. God needs to be the force behind all you do, the one directing and in control of where you are headed, the foundation upon which you build your life.

Why is God so important? Because He is life! Jesus says in John 11:25–26, "I am the resurrection and the life. He who believes in me will live, even though he dies; and whoever lives and believes in me will never die." And in John 15:5 Jesus describes Himself as the Vine with us growing out of Him as branches. Through Him flows life, and apart from Him we can do nothing. Jesus is the most important part of anything and everything you do, think, feel, and say.

Charles Allen in *God's Psychiatry* writes that "we are created incomplete . . . and we cannot be at rest until there's a satisfaction of our deepest hunger . . . the yearning of our souls."[1] What does your soul yearn for? What is it that will finally bring you rest? The answer is found in Scripture:

- "My soul yearns, even faints, for the courts of the LORD; my heart and my flesh cry out for the living God." Psalm 84:2
- "My soul finds rest in God alone." Psalm 62:1
- "As the deer pants for streams of water, so my soul pants for you, O God." Psalm 42:1
- "Whoever drinks the water I give him will never thirst. Indeed, the water I give him will become in him a spring of water welling up to eternal life." John 4:14
- "I am the bread of life. He who comes to me will never go hungry, and he who believes in me will never be thirsty." John 6:35

This deep craving that we have is for God, our Creator. This craving can only be filled through a personal relationship with Jesus Christ and through the spiritual food and drink He offers.

SEEK YE FIRST . . .

God knows that we need Him, and He promises to meet all of our needs if we seek Him first.

Christ addresses all the things of this world that we so often seek first instead of God. These are the things that most of us spend so much of our time worrying and fretting about. When earthly things come first on our list of priorities, we are never satisfied and therefore never get to anything else on the list. We no longer have the time or freedom to seek other things that we are hungering for. And the more earthly priorities scream to be filled, the more they drown out the Holy Spirit's beckoning us to Him. These out-of-control appetites begin to rob us of life and fellowship with God. And when that happens, our strongest need of all, our need for God, goes unfulfilled and our inner void grows bigger and more painful.

But there is hope! If we will fill our appetite for God first and foremost, all our other needs and appetites will be provided. It is when God is not our number-one priority that things get out of balance. That void we have inside really is a God-size void. Jesus says He will fill it to overflowing, and we will be satisfied when we seek Him first.

Unlike our physical appetite for food, we can never really get enough of God. Physical hunger signals us to eat, and when we do, we are satisfied. Once we experience this feeling of fullness, we no longer want or need food, or at least not until we become hungry again. As a matter of fact, we may be repulsed by the sight, smell, or even thought of food when our hunger for it is satisfied. Proverbs describes this physical phenomenon: "He who is full loathes honey, but to the hungry even what is bitter tastes sweet" (27:7). But this is not the case with our spiritual appetite.

Even as our appetite for God is satisfied, it is also intensified. He fills us up, yet we want more of Him. Matthew 5:6 says, "Blessed are those who hunger and thirst for righteousness, for they will be filled." There is a blessing connected to this craving for God. For many people this will be something new and different. If you have never actively sought out ways to feed your appetite for God, you may not realize how this appetite will develop.

If you have never tasted cheesecake, gone to a professional football game, played a card game with friends, or had sex, you don't know what you are missing and therefore probably don't have much of an appetite for those things. Not until you have experienced something

ARE YOU A SPIRITUAL ANOREXIC?

Although we have a natural, innate appetite for God and spiritual things, we may not be experiencing the sensations that would tell us we are hungering for Him. Why not? Maybe it's because we have been depriving ourselves of spiritual food for way too long. Are you refusing to feed yourself spiritually? If you don't actively seek God and instead ignore this yearning from deep inside, cravings can, and do, eventually change.

When we are physically hungry, our body sends us signals through our hunger pangs and cravings that tell us we need to eat. If ignored, these signals at first grow stronger in hopes of pushing us to fulfill the need for food. But if we continue to ignore this appetite for long enough, it will eventually begin to fade and we can actually convince ourselves that we really aren't hungry anymore. That is exactly what the anorexic does. She tells herself she isn't hungry and ignores the signals her body is sending her. Eventually she will have completely numbed her cravings to the point that she no longer desires food. She has so effectively convinced herself that she is not hungry that her body is now starving to death. Yet she doesn't even realize the danger. So too when we squelch our hunger for God.

This is how it can be with our spiritual appetite. When we are spiritually hungry, we experience the beckoning of the Holy Spirit within us to feast on the things of God. If we ignore our craving for God long enough, we will find the craving for Him eventually begins to fade. We are capable of convincing ourselves that we are doing "just fine," yet we are starving our spirit to the point of spiritual death. Our desires for the things of God fade, and we are no longer able to experience the draw of the Holy Spirit because we have so numbed ourselves to His call. Without even noticing it, prayer has become less important, we no longer thirst after God's Word, and we convince ourselves it's no big deal to miss church.

Both types of anorexics refuse themselves the nourishment they need to sustain life. The only way for both of them to heal and regain a healthy appetite that will help them grow is to pull up to the table and eat. Are you feasting at the banquet table of God? If you want to cultivate and grow your spiritual craving, you must feed it. Psalm 34:8 says, "Taste and see that the LORD is good." When you come to the banquet table to feast on the things of the Spirit, you will find that the Lord is good and that He satisfies completely. And, although the Lord does completely satisfy, once you taste of Him, you will find yourself wanting more and more of Him.

can you know if it is pleasurable to you and something that you would want more of. It is through the tasting of many different things that we develop our own personal set of activities we enjoy. Spiritually, we must taste God before we can possibly know if we will enjoy Him. Our cravings can change as a result of experiencing God. Someone who has never experienced a relationship with our Creator may say, "I have no desire for God," but how can they really know until they have tried Him? The reality is that the more we authentically experience God, the more we will desire Him.

Pursue these activities with great energy, even if you don't really feel like it. There may not be immediate, tangible results. But God is faithful to His children, and our efforts to know Him more will not go unnoticed.

STUDY GOD'S WORD

Through our study and knowledge of the Scripture, we can:

- Know God better (Ephesians 1:17–18)
- Gain wisdom and understanding (Psalm 119:130–33; Philippians 1:9–10)
- Avoid stumbling spiritually by resisting temptation and sin (Psalm 119:9–16)
- Find hope (Romans 15:4)
- Mature as Christians (Ephesians 4:13)
- Gain prosperity and success (Joshua 1:8)

Scripture says, "Your word is a lamp to my feet and a light for my path" (Psalm 119:105). The Bible is our map or instructional manual to godliness, and we need to keep it close by and read it often. Otherwise we will be walking in darkness and will surely stumble and fall. How hard we stumble and how far we fall may be determined by how long it has been since we have feasted on God's Word. The psalmist must have been doing this when he wrote, "How sweet are your words to my taste, sweeter than honey to my mouth!" (119:103). We need to feast on God's Word daily. Just as you need physical food each and every day to sustain your body, you also need spiritual food every day to sustain your soul.

DELIGHT IN THE LORD

Scripture tells us to "delight . . . in the LORD and he will give you the desires of your heart" (Psalm 37:4). Now be careful not to misinterpret this verse. This is *not* a magic wand to getting everything you want right now. Let's say you have a very strong desire to acquire, and what you want to acquire right now is a brand-new flat-screen TV, a new car, a boat, or any other materialistic possession. You read this verse and decide it must be your lucky day. Here you've been crunching numbers and trying to figure out how you can afford your newest toy, and all along God was just waiting for you to delight in Him and He would give you these desires of your heart, right? That just is not true. If you cannot afford a material possession and you are truly delighting yourself in the Lord, then the desires of your heart change to what you can afford. Only an immature Christian would see God as a magician whose purpose is to provide you with things that would only serve to distract you from God.

As the new Christian begins the process of delighting in the Lord (for the purpose of getting what he wants), he starts spending more and more time with God. And do you know what spending time with God does to us? It changes us from the inside out. Before he realizes it, what he once so strongly desired has changed because his heart has changed. He has grown closer to God, who has renewed his mind and filled his heart with new desires for things not of this world but things that have eternal value. Through delighting in the Lord, we become new creatures with new hearts filled with new desires that God promises to richly fulfill. And that's how we mature as Christians. We draw closer to God and become more like Him, desiring the very things He desires for us.

What does it mean to delight in the Lord? Let's consider what it would mean if you had a friend you delighted in. What would that be like? Most likely, you would spend time with her, talk often together, and look forward to your time together as you let her into your life and your world. That is exactly how we can delight in God. Through our reading of His Word, our prayers and meditation, and our worship of Him, we build a relationship with God in which we delight in Him.

Reading God's Word is studying what He has written to learn more about Him. It's like reading a friend's letters over and over. But prayer and meditation are even more personal than that. It is your face-to-face time with your friend. This is where you really experience each other. Prayer and meditation is the two-way communication that takes place between you and God that draws you ever closer to each other. Prayer is your turn to talk, and meditation is God's turn to talk.

Have you ever been in a relationship where the other person does all the talking? Sometimes you become such a good listener that the other person feels great comfort and ease in sharing personal problems and conflicts with you. The more a person shares with you, the greater the connection they will feel with you. Many have had the experience of someone identifying them as their best friend and not feeling the same way toward that person. How does this happen?

So think about how this might play out in our relationship with Christ. Is the time we spend with Him consumed by us doing all the talking? Are we sharing with Him from the depths of our pain and needing help, guidance and wisdom from Him, but then never taking time to really listen to Him? Are we giving Him time to share about Himself and His desires with us? Do we ever really take time to be the listener? If we don't, we very likely may be the only one in the relationship who considers the other to be their "best friend." Many of us call Jesus our best friend, but how many of us would Jesus call His best friends? Our relationship with Jesus won't grow unless there is equal time for talking (prayer) and listening (meditation). It is in the combination of these two parts of conversation that results in the fullness of communing with God and becoming best friends.

As we learn to communicate more fully with God, we mature spiritually. And spiritual maturity results in our desires changing from carnal to eternal. Jesus tells us that "where your treasure is, there your heart will be also" (Matthew 6:21). As baby Christians, we will struggle to understand this because our focus is still in this world. But as we mature and these things become the desires of our heart, we begin to understand what Jesus was teaching.

BELIEVE HIS PROMISES

From the first page to the last, Scripture is filled with promises that God has made to us. He loves us and wants wonderful things for us, yet we struggle to believe that God really will do what He says He will do. As we cultivate our divine appetites, we should take great comfort from His promises.

He is always near and will never forsake you. "For the LORD loves the just and will not forsake his faithful ones. They will be protected forever" (Psalm 37:28).

He watches over you and cares for you. "He will not let your foot slip—he who watches over you will not slumber; indeed, he who watches over Israel will neither slumber nor sleep. The LORD watches over you—the LORD is your shade at your right hand; the sun will not harm you by day, nor the moon by night. The LORD will keep you from all harm—he will watch over your life; the LORD will watch over your coming and going both now and forevermore" (Psalm 121:3–8).

He has good plans for you. "For I know the plans I have for you," declares the LORD, "plans to prosper you and not to harm you, plans to give you hope and a future" (Jeremiah 29:11).

He will listen when you pray and seek Him. "Then you will call upon me and come and pray to me, and I will listen to you. You will seek me and find me when you seek me with all your heart"(Jeremiah 29:12–13).

He will give you strength. "You are awesome, O God, in your sanctuary; the God of Israel gives power and strength to his people. Praise be to God!" (Psalm 68:35).

He will forgive you when you fail. "Who is a God like you, who pardons sin and forgives the transgression of the remnant of his inheritance? You do not stay angry forever but delight to show mercy" (Micah 7:18).

EXPERIENCE FELLOWSHIP WITH THE BODY

God encourages us through Scripture to spend time together with other believers. "And let us consider how we may spur one another on toward love and good deeds. Let us not give up meeting together, as some are in the habit of doing, but let us encourage one another —and all the more as you see the Day approaching" (Hebrews 10:24–25). As you seek to grow closer to God and to feed your divine appetite, we encourage you to find a local church that you are comfortable with and start spending time with them, growing healthy relationships that will in turn grow you.

There are several obvious reasons that God encourages us to spend time together. He knows how easily His children can be influenced by the world and therefore drawn away from Him. So He provides us with friends and family who believe and behave in similar ways to help fill our need to be with people. If He had not provided those people, we would still have the need to feel we belong to a group; therefore, we would be hanging with people whose lives would not mirror what God hopes ours to be. Stephen Apthorp writes, "God offers us life. He calls us to share that life, to live in meaningful relationships with others and, especially, with Him. Abundant life is not found in instant gratification. It comes when we seek a meaningful relation with God, which in turn is self-fulfilling and fosters more wholesome relationships with others."[2] These meaningful, healthy, and wholesome relationships that will best fulfill us are the ones we develop with other believers.

But our relationships with other believers also serve as a basis for support, encouragement, and accountability. Scripture says, "Carry each other's burdens, and in this way you will fulfill the law of Christ" (Galatians 6:2). When we are having a rough time in our lives, it's important to know we aren't alone. Showing we support each other through these rough times is what God's family is all about. But we are not to just be together when things are not going well. Scripture also addresses sharing our joy with each other. "Rejoice with those who rejoice; mourn with those who mourn" (Romans 12:15). It's been said that fellowshiping together divides the sorrows and mul-tiplies the joys. What a wonderful thing God has provided for us through our spiritual family.

Being in close contact with other believers brings many opportunities to encourage each other. Hebrews 3:13 says, "But encourage one another daily, as long as it is called Today, so that none of you may be hardened by sin's deceitfulness." We can't encourage each other if we don't take the time to get to know each other in such a way that we feel comfortable sharing our needs.

Experiencing God's people will also help us as we grow spiritually through the process of accountability. At one time or another, each one of us wants to stray in search of our own fulfillment. Knowing that someone is going to check on us and ask us if we are doing what we need to be doing will remind us that we are loved and cared for. It is difficult to move too far away from God's plan when we feel accountable.

One final benefit of experiencing God's people is described in 1 John 4:11–12: "Dear friends, since God so loved us, we also ought to love one another. No one has ever seen God; but if we love one another, God lives in us and his love is made complete in us." Through our love for one another, we demonstrate Christ's love to the world around us. Our love for the body of Christ not only benefits us individually, but it becomes a significant witness to unbelievers who are watching how we demonstrate our love for our spiritual brothers and sisters.

SHARE IN HIS WORK

Growing closer to God includes becoming interested in what God is interested in. If you want to work with God, you will need to know what kind of business He's in. God is in the "people business." Everything He does centers around people. He wants to support them, provide for them, bless them, protect them, love them, forgive them, and most of all, bring them closer to Him. That's what God does. And if we want to join Him in His work, that is what we need to learn to do. Jesus commands us, "Love each other as I have loved you. Greater love has no one than this, that he lay down his life for his friends. You are my friends if you do what I command. I no longer call you servants, because a servant does not know his master's business. Instead, I have called you friends, for everything that I learned from my Father I have made known to you" (John 15:12–15).

Jesus has made His business known to us and has set the example before us. What we choose to do is up to us. But, if we want to fulfill and grow our appetite for Him, we will go about His business of loving and serving others.

Jesus modeled for his disciples the importance of serving others by washing their feet in the upper room (see John 13:1–17). After He had done this, He said, "Now that I, your Lord and Teacher, have washed your feet, you also should wash one another's feet. I have set you an example that you should do as I have done for you" (vv. 14–15). How do we go about doing as He did? Do we need to actually sit people down and wash their feet? No, but it might not be a bad idea. Serving others is about focusing more on their needs than on your own. It's about putting them first. Anything you do for another person as an act of service is like serving Christ Himself.

> For I was hungry and you gave me something to eat, I was thirsty and you gave me something to drink, I was a stranger and you invited me in, I needed clothes and you clothed me, I was sick and you looked after me, I was in prison and you came to visit me.

Then the righteous will answer him, "Lord, when did we see you hungry and feed you, or thirsty and give you something to drink? When did we see you a stranger and invite you in, or needing clothes and clothe you? When did we see you sick or in prison and go to visit you?"

The King will reply, "I tell you the truth, whatever you did for one of the least of these brothers of mine, you did for me." (Matthew 25:35–40)

When we take the time to be a part of the work God is doing for the people of this world, we not only please God and help a fellow brother feel better, but we also help ourselves. Focusing attention on the needs of others will tend to make us feel more productive and will therefore increase our overall sense of self-worth. God's kingdom is full of such opportunities for service and ministry.

As we read the following story of one man's struggle to control an appetite for gambling, note the action he takes to ultimately succeed in fighting this desire. As Shawn found, nourishing an appetite for ministry and personal spiritual growth helps to replace the destructive appetite that previously held us in bondage. A peace that passes all understanding awaits us if we surrender ourselves to our Lord's calling and commit to active service in His earthly kingdom.

"There Is Peace"

By the time Shawn sought help, his world was falling in all around him. He was thirty-three years old and had gone from being a man who appeared to have it all to a man about to lose everything that was really important to him. For most of his marriage of eleven years, life had appeared to be going well. Together he and Angie had three beautiful children, and Shawn was a partner in a successful law firm with a thriving practice. But it didn't seem like enough to Shawn. He wasn't able to fulfill his inner void. He wanted more. It was the desire for the unattainable that took him to the brink of personal disaster.

"I had been living two completely separate lives and hiding it well for many years," Shawn said as he tried to explain what had gotten him to the edge of this cliff. "I always tried to be the 'good kid' growing up because I didn't like what I saw happen to my older brother when he wasn't 'good.' I learned how to please others, look good on the outside, and then do what I wanted when no one was watching. I became an overachiever and soon realized that achievements became a protection that allowed me to do even more in my other life. People are much less likely to question your activities when you are successful and providing financially. I learned to lie to protect my secret life and to keep up the façade if it were ever at risk. But now the lies have caught up with me, and my two worlds have collided and I have lost it all."

Shawn had started gambling occasionally as a young teen with his allowance "just for fun" and found that he liked the feeling he would get with a win. This behavior seemed innocent, but as he grew up he never forgot the feeling it produced. When he was twenty-two years old, Shawn went to his first casino and ended up staying there all night and spent more money than he had planned to. There was a sense of pleasure and excitement, but not an overwhelming urge to return at that point. He lived in Missouri, which was nowhere close to a casino, so there was little opportunity to return anytime soon to his favorite pastime. Distance from the source of his thrills helped him stay in control until he found out that a neighboring state had gambling at the dog tracks. What he thought would do no harm started him down a path to total destruction.

Shawn's urge to gamble started to grow, and he became secretive about his activities. He began to max out his credit cards and then hope for the big win to pay them off before Angie found out—which often happened just in the nick of time. This only intensified the adrenaline rush that he so enjoyed and reinforced his appetite for risking it all. Each time he returned to the tables, the power and thrill were intoxicating. Then the unthinkable happened. Casinos became legal not only in his home state, but right in his hometown. "It was all downhill from there," Shawn shared. He explained that for the next couple of years his gambling increased, as did his lies, deceit, and cover-up. The money he was making from his law practice was all going to support his habit and his family was living on Angie's income and credit cards and loans from a bank and a few naive friends.

Eventually the "big win" didn't come when it was so desperately needed, and Shawn had to tell Angie about his problem, which was now their problem. She was devastated and hurt, her trust of him had been broken, and Shawn knew he would have to make some changes. He committed to Angie that they would start over and he would find a new way.

They filed bankruptcy and moved three hours away from Kansas

City as a deterrent. He made all the promises he could to help Angie begin to trust him again. Things seemed to really be better . . . for a while. After Shawn got his practice established with new partners, and his family settled, he found himself becoming unsettled all over again. Everything was beginning to look pretty good from the outside, but inside he was dying. He missed the thrill of the win and the adrenaline rush the casinos seemed to provide. He had forgotten the pain that came along with it (or at least pushed those memories away). Shawn started looking for opportunities to go out of town "on business" whenever he possibly could. His slide back into the compulsion was very quick.

He became even more secretive and deceptive in how he got his gambling money and in covering his tracks. But before he knew it, Shawn was right back where he had been, only this time the debt was deeper when he got caught. Again he saw his problem for what it was and wanted badly to change. He didn't like who he was becoming and took firm measures to stop himself. He and Angie set up their finances so he didn't have access to their bank accounts, and Shawn asked that Angie take charge of all the household finances. This time he really wanted to change!

Shawn's commitment to change lasted for about one week. He found a loophole and got around the safeguards that had been put in place. He was a little frustrated at times that the money was not so easily accessible, but it didn't stop him. Eventually his desire for gambling, his main source for fulfillment, became so strong that it drove him to illegal means of gaining the money necessary to fill his void.

Shawn was the custodian of several estates for elderly people who were in various stages of decline. He had power of attorney and could make out checks to their caregivers, pay taxes, and other purchase expenses. In desperation, he set up a false healthcare company and began writing checks out of the accounts that were under his protection. In Shawn's mind, this was not an illegal scheme to hurt these elderly people; instead, he was merely loaning himself money until he would win it back and return the funds to their accounts with interest.

The "need" to gamble seemed to grow bigger and bigger the more Shawn fed it. The void he was trying to fill seemed only temporarily satisfied when he got away to gamble, but then would return with a vengeance. He was out of control and often could not work because the obsession with gambling was so great. He didn't know how to stop. The drive was so big, it became easier to just give in rather than to attempt to fight it only to end up giving in later. He knew he was headed for a crash but just kept convincing himself that he would find his game, get back on a winning streak, and make everything okay. Then he could stop.

But that didn't happen.

Shawn's world came crashing in when one of the estates he managed performed an audit and discovered that much of the money Shawn was supposed to be handling was gone. The estate turned over the evidence to a local prosecutor, and charges were filed. Shawn was removed from the law practice and immediately was without any source of income. He didn't have the money to pay back what he had taken, and the only solution he could come up with was to get "one more big win." So off to the casino he went. But that isn't where he ended up. He was arrested, handcuffed, and taken to jail. Charges were filed, and there was no money to post bond. He had to stay in jail until his trial. At his trial Shawn was found guilty of a felony, sent to prison for two years, and disbarred. His wife had to work full time to support the family and pay off his debts. The only thing harder than Angie having to work and parent their children alone was her need to work through her anger toward Shawn. But she did, and she became an encourager to Shawn. They would begin again.

Although Shawn experienced significant consequences for his choices, he has found a new and complete source of fulfillment. It was through this experience that Shawn realized his complete and utter need for God as his source of fulfillment. His attempt to fill a void inside himself with the adrenaline that gambling provided did nothing but leave him in more pain. Yet eventually it drove him to his knees to seek God to fill that void. And God has now filled that void completely.

Without God in his life, Shawn had become totally self absorbed. People he had once loved had meant nothing to him while he gambled. He had disconnected from everyone and instead used those closest to him to support his gambling. He began to surrender to God, he started to see other people, connect with them, and even help them.

While in prison, Shawn became a leader for Prison Fellowship. While he could not practice law on the outside, he could on the inside. Shawn began to look at the cases of his fellow prisoners. He helped them with appeals and became engrossed with this service for others. Together they celebrated their victories and shared their losses. He became a caring and loving human being who was now free from the bondage of an addictive appetite. Ironically, although he had never looked worse to the world at large, Shawn now felt better about life and his contribution to it than ever before.

The last two years have been difficult, but at the same time, this period has been the most growth-producing time of his life. God has proven Himself faithful and able to strengthen Shawn to make healthier choices. Shawn is learning healthy and appropriate ways to handle his need for adrenaline rushes. He is seeking God through Bible study, ministry activities, and in service to others. He has an active prayer life. He is sharing his story both as a witness for what God can do and as an accountability tool. His marriage to Angie is solid—his wife still loves him and they have a new life together. To Shawn, life now looks right and feels right. Where once deceit and uncertainty clouded his life, he now has peace of mind, something he had not experienced prior to this experience.

I SURRENDER ALL

All to Jesus, I surrender; All to Him I freely give;
I will ever love and trust Him, In His presence daily live.

I surrender all, I surrender all,
All to Thee, my blessed Savior, I surrender all.

All to Jesus I surrender; Humbly at His feet I bow,
Worldly pleasures all forsaken; Take me, Jesus, take me now.

I surrender all, I surrender all,
All to Thee, my blessed Savior, I surrender all.

All to Jesus, I surrender; Make me, Savior, wholly Thine;
Let me feel the Holy Spirit, Truly know that Thou art mine.

I surrender all, I surrender all,
All to Thee, my blessed Savior, I surrender all.

All to Jesus, I surrender; Lord, I give myself to Thee;
Fill me with Thy love and power; Let Thy blessing fall on me.

I surrender all, I surrender all,
All to Thee, my blessed Savior, I surrender all.

All to Jesus I surrender; Now I feel the sacred flame.
O the joy of full salvation! Glory, glory, to His Name!

I surrender all, I surrender all,
All to Thee, my blessed Savior, I surrender all.

—JUDSON W. VAN DE VENTER, 1896

10

THE
SURRENDERED LIFE

*S*URRENDER. Many of us have heard this word in church, but we don't know what it means or how to go about doing it, or even how essential it really is to living a life pleasing to God. Webster's Dictionary describes *surrender* as "to give up possession of; to give oneself up."[1] As Christians we are taught to surrender ourselves to Christ, but we may not be taught *how* to do that. We know there is surrender when we commit our lives to Christ. Yet living our lives in continual surrender is more than a one-time decision. It becomes a daily part of our existence and shapes our entire world-view.

A Christian believes that salvation (choosing to believe in and accept Jesus Christ as our personal Savior) is the essential element to eternal life in heaven. The Christian also believes that living a godly life here on earth requires a daily willingness to let go of anything that may be standing in the way of us and the Creator. It is inviting Jesus in and asking the Holy Spirit to guide our lives and empower us to make the right decisions no matter how tough they are.

Many Christians have chosen Jesus as their Savior and stopped there. But if we really want to live a life pleasing to God, and if we want to let the Holy Spirit work through us, we must take another step. We must make Jesus not just *Savior,* but also *Lord* of our lives. What's the difference? Accepting him as Savior means that we understand we are sinners and deserve death as a result of our sin. It involves accepting that Jesus made the ultimate sacrifice by dying on the cross to take away our sins. Through our belief in him we gain eternal life.

But when we make Jesus the Lord of our life, we surrender our will, desires, plans, and possessions, everything we have, to Him. He gets *all* of us to do with as He sees fit. Making Jesus Lord means that we don't hold anything back from Him. We don't give Him part of us and hang on to the rest to do with as we choose. True surrender means trusting Him enough to let Him take over control of our lives. God is in the driver's seat and takes us where He wants, when He wants, and the way He wants. There is no backseat driving when we are truly surrendered. "Surrender is admitting that we can't handle life without God. We stop pretending to be God, get off the throne of our lives, and let God rule. In short, surrender means to obey him. We come to God on his terms, accepting that he is God and that he can do with us whatever he wants; but trusting that because he is a God of love, whatever he wants to do with us will be for our ultimate good."[2]

TRUST AND OBEY

"Trust and obey, for there's no other way to be happy in Jesus but to trust and obey." The words of that familiar hymn resound with the essential elements of surrender. We must learn to trust and obey God if we are going to surrender our lives to Him. "For it is God who works in you to will and to act according to his good purpose" (Philippians 2:13). If we don't trust that God loves us and wants good things for us, we are not likely to surrender our will to Him. Studying Scripture and gaining understanding of who God really is will help us to better trust Him as we hand our lives over.

Can you imagine saying you were surrendered to someone but had no intention of actually obeying him? Let's look at what Jesus has to say about obedience:

> If you love me, you will obey what I command. . . . Whoever has my commands and obeys them, he is the one who loves me. He who loves me will be loved by my Father, and I too will love him and show myself to him. . . . Jesus replied, "If anyone loves me, he will obey my teaching. My Father will love him, and we will come to him and make our home with him. He who does not love me will not obey my teaching. These words you hear are not my own; they belong to the Father who sent me. (John 14:15, 21, 23–24)

The importance of obeying God's commands is stated often in Scripture, and almost always, the act of obedience is paired with a blessing of some sort or another (Leviticus 25:18; Deuteronomy 4:29–31; 6:3; Jeremiah 7:23). When we choose to do what God tells us to do, things will go well for us and God will bless us: "Blessed rather are those who hear the word of God and obey it" (Luke 11:28).

SUCCESS THROUGH THE SPIRIT

Even after salvation and making the choice to surrender to Christ as Lord of our life, we will still face struggles and trials in regard to controlling our appetites. We tend to fall back easily into old patterns that are focused on our flesh instead of the Spirit that lives within us. The urges we faced before surrendering to Christ will still present themselves, at least for a while, but now we don't have to face this battle alone. The Holy Spirit is there to strengthen us.

There are times when these temptations will feel so strong we will be tempted to say, "I can't make it through this one." And you may be right. But here's the hope: *you* don't have to. Once you have accepted Jesus as your Savior, He lives within you. According to Scripture, "I have been crucified with Christ and I no longer live, but Christ lives in me. The life I live in the body, I live by faith in the Son of God, who loved me and gave himself for me" (Galatians 2:20). If we have been crucified with Christ, we are dead to ourselves and what lives within us now is the Spirit of God. First Corinthians 10:13 says, "No temptation has seized you except what is common to man. And God is faithful; he will not let you be tempted beyond what you can bear. But when you are tempted, he will also provide a way out so that you can stand up under it."

Jesus Christ lives in us and promises to help us resist temptation and to strengthen us to surrender and do His will. The Lord will never ask you to do something you can't do. Why? Because if we truly have died to self and have Christ living within us, then it is really Him being asked to do whatever it is. Furthermore, we know we "can do everything through him who gives me strength" (Philippians 4:13). We *can* control our appetites. As you embark on this challenge to surrender, we recommend that you engage some outside help in the form of a trusted friend or professional counselor or a self-help or support group.

You must be willing to let go of control and to surrender to the help your counselor offers. Don't try to control the therapist, the direction of therapy, or even yourself. Control is an attempt to exert power, and

A NOTE TO THE STILL-FRUSTRATED

Now that you are nearing the end of the book you may feel frustrated because you did not have a life-changing experience while reading it. Perhaps the walls didn't come tumbling down, lights didn't flash along your reading road, and you still feel pretty much the same as when you started.

It's okay. You're in the majority because change doesn't usually come from simply reading a book. But this could be the beginning of changes that lead to a new life for you. It all begins with taking the first step. You have effectively done that by reading this book this far. If you continue on to the end of this book and try to implement some or all the twelve steps listed in the Appendix, the journey to fulfilling your appetites will continue. The implementation of one new change can create a momentum that will lead you to more changes.

If you are frustrated, view it as a really good sign. Frustration comes from being one way yet knowing there is another way, a better way. We hope this truly will be a new beginning for you. If the urge to do whatever you have been doing overwhelms you, please, get up and get out of the house. It doesn't matter whether you go to a meeting of friends, a support-group meeting, or merely to visit someone in need. If you can't get out of the house, pick up the phone and call a friend. Start that conversation with a simple admission of needing to talk, of needing some assurance.

This is how life change begins for most people. Over a long period of time, small changes lead you to connect to people in new, deeper, and richer ways. So if you are frustrated, move on and take a baby step into a new life.

real power comes from God. As you surrender to the treatment process and begin to work through your pain, you will find relief from the very pain that has held you hostage. Through the power of the Holy Spirit, you can begin to control yourself and your appetites. With increased self-control will come increased self-confidence and freedom from the need or desire to control others. Surrender yourself to God and take this step to healthy, victorious living.

Why not start today? What better time to start taking control of your appetites than right now? Focus on taking this journey just one day at a time. Your battle for control happens one day at a time and starts fresh each day. Don't look back at the time you have missed, and don't focus on how long it is going to take. Just do what you have committed to do each and every day and watch as God blesses your efforts.

If you need assistance in finding a Christian counselor or other resource in your area you can phone 1-800-NEW-LIFE anytime, night or day.
Please visit our Web sites at Newlife.com and LoseItForLife.com.

APPENDIX:
TWELVE STEPS TO SUCCESSFULLY FEEDING YOUR APPETITES

We are so proud of you! You have read the book and are ready for the next step. To successfully change your situation, you need to know where those changes should be made. Evaluating your circumstances will give you a map clearly showing the areas where you are struggling. Please be honest with yourself. Your ability to change depends on a realistic approach for what will work best for *you*.

APPENDIX

1. Make a list of the areas where you are not demonstrating self-control. Consider the appetite(s) you are dealing with, even if your struggle is only moderate. Don't get overwhelmed by this list— you are not going to try to fix them all at once. Keep in mind that appetites run deeper than the more obvious ones covered in the book, such as food or power. Search yourself for appetites for safety, disconnection, manipulation, superiority, and victimization. Digging deeper into these more hidden appetites will help you as you work on the more obvious ones.

_____

2. Make a list of the lies you have been telling yourself. This may be a little more difficult than your first list because you are now facing the reality that you have made excuses to make yourself feel better and to allow yourself to continue in an unhealthy pattern. Be sure to include both the lies and excuses you have told yourself that have precipitated your unhealthy use of your appetites.

- "I don't deserve to be loved."
- "I'll never amount to anything."
- "I'm damaged goods."

_____

_____

_____

_____

_____

_____

Also, include those lies and excuses you have used to continue your negative pattern.

- "I really love him, so sex is okay."
- "I can stop this whenever I want to. I just don't want to."
- "Everyone's doing it."

Putting these lies down on paper may make them seem much more ridiculous than they sounded in your head. The hope is that as you become aware of your lies, you will be much less willing to use them to excuse your behaviors.

_____

_____

_____

_____

_____

_____

3. Evaluate your self-talk. All of us talk to ourselves, but we are not always aware of what we are really saying. You will need to start becoming more aware of what you are saying to yourself because your self-talk can have a big influence on how you feel and act. If you are constantly cutting yourself down and criticizing yourself, either in your head or out loud to others, you will have difficulty liking yourself or believing that you are capable of successfully making the necessary changes. However, if you are positive about yourself and your ability to change, you are halfway there.

Start noticing the negative things you are saying to yourself. Write these statements down. Then make a list of more positive statements you can start replacing the negative thoughts with. For example, if you find yourself saying, "It's hopeless. I'll never get this under control," identify it as negative self-talk and write it down. Then find a healthier statement to replace the negative one, such as, "I know if I really commit to this, I can make a change."

_____

_____

_____

_____

_____

_____

_____

_____

_____

_____

_____

_____

4. Make a list of healthy activities that bring you pleasure. And we do mean *all* the things that bring you pleasure! Include the small day-to-day things that make you smile as well as bigger events you look forward to. The more items you can come up with the better. This list is going to help retrain your brain. The more you can engage in the things you enjoy that are healthy for you, the more your brain will push you to act on these activities in times of stress so that the old, unhealthy behaviors remain a thing of the past.

You might be at a place where it is difficult to think of what gives you pleasure. If that is the case, perhaps this list of healthy appetites will spur you on to think of other areas of life you enjoy: giving, serving, connecting, loving, saving, fitness, family, peace, joy, music, art, worship, prayer, meditation, Bible study, and any other activities you enjoy.

_____

_____

_____

_____

_____

_____

_____

_____

_____

_____

_____

_____

_____

_____

5. Confess, repent, and seek. Before you will be able to grow spiritually, you must remove all barriers that stand between you and God. You must admit that you have been struggling with controlling your appetites and that these activities may very likely be sinful. As you identify these sins in your life, you must confess and repent (decide to stop doing it). When you do this, your relationship with God is restored and He is available to help you. Take time to seek the help of the Holy Spirit by asking for the strength and power necessary to make these changes.

6. Grow in wisdom, knowledge, and understanding. If you hope to become more Christlike, you must know what Christ is like. You must study God's Word on a daily basis and do your best to commit portions of it to memory so you will have it readily available to you when temptations come. It is through God's Word that we gain an understanding of what He commands us to do, how the Holy Spirit works in our lives, and the promises God provides to us. God's Word is our instructional manual for handling the tough situations that come our way. Study it!

_____

_____

_____

_____

_____

_____

_____

_____

_____

_____

_____

_____

_____

_____

_____

_____

_____

7. Draw closer to God. There are two major benefits to drawing closer to God. First, as we draw closer to God and really work to get to know Him through spending time with Him, we will begin to see sin and the things of this world as they really are. Satan's schemes will be exposed, and we will be less deceived. We will no longer want what the devil is offering because we are now full of what God provides. The second benefit is that as we get to know and trust God more, we will notice that we are being transformed to a closer likeness of Him. As that happens, our desires will change to match what His desires are for us.

8. Engage in spiritual warfare. See the enemy for who he is and fight him with the weapons you have been given. Stop being deceived either through temptations or by believing that you are powerless in this battle. Remember, you are a child of the King, and He has made everything available to you to succeed in this fight with the enemy.

9. Take control of your thoughts. One of the most difficult things you may ever attempt to do is to learn to control your thoughts. Regardless of how difficult this can be, it is also one of the most necessary steps if you want to change how you are acting. The battle you are facing begins in the mind. If you learn to control your thoughts, your battle can end right there. The problem most of us have in this area of thought control is that we don't catch our thoughts soon enough.

Many thoughts that will eventually turn negative may start out seemingly innocent and therefore be dismissed as "no big deal." But this is part of Satan's deception. If he can get us to entertain the little thoughts, then he can gradually grow them bigger and bigger right under our noses. Philippians 4:8 tells us, "Finally, brothers, whatever is true, whatever is noble, whatever is right, whatever is pure, whatever is lovely, whatever is admirable—if anything is excellent or praiseworthy—think about such things." Wrong thinking cannot lead to right doing. We must have right thinking if we want to engage in right doing.

10. Determine to work on one appetite at a time. One of the biggest culprits to being unsuccessful in making changes comes in the form of becoming overwhelmed. If we look at our lives and focus on the entire list of things that need to be changed, we may become so overwhelmed that we give up before we ever get started.

Pick one appetite in which you would like to see yourself demonstrating more self-control and start there. Put any others you listed in the first exercise away, and don't start on them until you have achieved sufficient success on the one you chose.

_____
_____
_____
_____
_____
_____
_____
_____
_____
_____
_____
_____
_____
_____
_____
_____
_____
_____
_____

11. Stop feeding your flesh. This is where the rubber meets the road. Make a plan of action as to how you will go about changing your behavior to now fulfill this appetite in a healthy way. Be sure that the goals you set are realistic and that you give yourself a sufficient amount of time to see change. Remember, you didn't get to this place overnight, and you won't get out of it that way either. Some psychological research has shown that it takes approximately twenty-one days to break an old habit and form a new one.[1] So be patient with yourself.

_____

_____

_____

_____

_____

_____

_____

_____

_____

_____

_____

_____

_____

_____

_____

_____

_____

_____

_____

_____

_____

_____

12. Discover your state when your appetite is under control. Every person has a state of mind or multiple states of mind where they find themselves in control of their appetites. Each of these states is the result of a surrendered heart.

Contentment is the emotional and spiritual condition exemplified by the apostle Paul. A man held captive in prison, during his life he was beaten, shipwrecked, and robbed, amid many other horrible happenings. In the midst of all this adversity, Paul was content. To him it mattered little whether he had a little or a lot. It is with contentment, satisfaction, and the acceptance of a tough reality that we may keep our appetites under control and in perspective to the other areas of our lives.

Look at your life. Examine yourself. Discover where you are in control of your longings and impulsive urges and reflect on how you feel. Determine to spread those feelings to all areas of your life.

_____

_____

_____

_____

_____

_____

_____

_____

_____

_____

_____

_____

_____

_____

_____

STUDY GUIDE

Chapter 1: The Quest for Fulfillment

1. Define the word "fulfillment." Next, define the concept of "appetite" as it will be used in this study.

    _____

    _____

    _____

    _____

2. What happens when a person has an unsatisfied desire and cannot fulfill his needs?

    _____

    _____

    _____

    _____

3. Did you complete the self-evaluation questions at the end of the chapter on page 10? Write your responses here.

_____
_____
_____
_____

4. Read Psalm 17, noting the last two verses in particular. How can the psalmist approach God with such certainty that he will be satisfied? Do you have that same comfort?

_____
_____
_____
_____

Chapter 2: What God Intended

1. Is it difficult to think of your appetites as being good? Explain.

_____
_____
_____
_____

2. Did any of the eight appetites' beginnings that were covered in this chapter surprise you in any way? Which would you consider your primary "problem" appetite? Why?

_____
_____
_____

3. Read Ecclesiastes 2:24–26. Does this passage make you feel uncomfortable?

_____

_____

_____

_____

4. Trace the path your problem appetite has followed in your own life. Can you see the good, original purpose behind that appetite? At what point did it begin to be a problem?

_____

_____

_____

_____

Chapter 3: The Choice Factor

1. Name one activity that gives you pleasure. Are you ashamed to admit it to yourself? To God? Describe the pleasure you receive. Is it instant? Lasting? Ultimately have the potential to hurt you? Others?

_____

_____

_____

_____

2. When faced with an unhealthy choice to satisfy a desire, do you view the instance as a battle of the flesh? How does this concept change how you view and combat unhealthy choices?

_____

_____

_____

_____

3. Study James 1:12–15. Describe this process in regard to a recent instance with your problem appetite, tracing the initial desire, an enticement, and eventually the sinful result. What awaits the Christian who fights temptation?

_____

_____

_____

_____

4. Does your mind have Scripture to meditate on when an appetite rages out of control? Spend some time in the Word; find three Scriptures that speak to a believer's need for self-control and the reward for reigning in unhealthy desires. Consider memorizing at least one of them.

_____

_____

_____

_____

_____

Chapter 4: How Change Begins

1. Define "forgiveness." Read Psalm 130. Do you feel uplifted and encouraged? Why or why not?

_____

_____

_____

_____

2. Is there a lie that tricked you into rationalizing your previous behavior? How will you combat it in the future?

_____

_____

_____

_____

3. If you are ready to change, the time has come to take a big step. Make a plan of action for how and when you will seek to reconcile with God and ask the forgiveness of those whom you have hurt while fulfilling your appetite. (Don't forget to make an appointment to forgive yourself too!)

_____

_____

_____

_____

4. What steps will you take in your efforts to remove temptation from your life and actively seek change? Write out a purpose statement for your life as you begin anew.

_____

_____

_____

_____

Chapter 5: Introduction to Influences

1. Name three influences in this chapter that you could relate to in your own appetite battle. Describe how each influence has affected your thought process as you fight temptation.

_____

_____

_____

_____

2. What does your brain use/recommend to help bring balance to your body when you are stressed? Does that choice satisfy? Or are you still hungry or in need of a "fix"?

_____

_____

_____

_____

3. Evaluate what is behind the appetite you are battling—are you lonely? Unhappy? Disappointed? Grieving? Dig deep and analyze those feelings that bring you to desire and the feelings that result when you satisfy an appetite. Write it all down, even if it is painful.

_____

_____

_____

_____

4. Read Romans 8:5–27 and meditate over the miracle of a life lived in the Spirit. Do you too rejoice in this declaration of Paul? How will this passage help you when the next battle comes?

_____

_____

_____

_____

Chapter 6: Filling the Void (Times Eight)

1. The prophet Jeremiah speaks of a satisfied God-appetite: "When your words came, I ate them; they were my joy and my heart's delight, for I bear your name, O LORD God Almighty." Do you hunger after God's Word?

_____

_____

_____

_____

2. Are you feeling hopeless as your problem appetite yearns to be satisfied? Seek your heavenly Father first before giving into past patterns. Nothing is too big for Him to heal. Write down one previous experience when you gave in to your appetite's cravings in the past. Did that choice bring lasting comfort or satisfaction?

_____

_____

_____

_____

3. Study the following Scriptures. What promises does God make to His children?

   Matthew 5:6

_____

_____

_____

_____

   Luke 6:21

_____

_____

_____

_____

   Revelation 7:15–17

_____

_____

_____

_____

Chapter 7: Fruit in All Its Forms

1. How can we bear fruit? (See John 15:1–8).

   _____

   _____

   _____

   _____

2. What is God's remedy for victory over temptation? (Galatians 5:16–17).

   _____

   _____

   _____

   _____

3. As this chapter tells us, we can respond to a situation by appealing to our physical, rational, or spiritual nature. When faced with your own problem appetite, what is your initial response? Why?

   _____

   _____

   _____

   _____

4. Although Christ is our sustenance, many believers have substituted other things for the true Vine. Since becoming a Christian, have you gravitated toward trusting more in something else? If so, what? Resolve to confess this sin and to seek God for your security.

_____

_____

_____

_____

Chapter 8: New Pathways

1. Note the diagram on page 130. Using a recent experience with your problem appetite, draw this diagram and include the specific instances of how you restricted yourself, the point when your appetite screamed to be fed, how and when you responded by "feeding" it excessively, and when and how you sought to gain control again.

_____

_____

_____

_____

2. Is seeking pleasure through indulgence wrong? Why or why not?

_____

_____

_____

_____

3. List three new methods or alternative activities from the chapter you intend to try in order to restore balance in your life through healthy, God-honoring means.

_____

_____

_____

_____

Chapter 9: Cultivating a Divine Appetite

1. How big is your commitment to God? Make a list of the activities you do during the week. Next to each item, note which ones are done for you and which ones are done out of love and service for God? Are you happy with the results of this exercise?

_____

_____

_____

_____

2. What does it mean to make no place for the devil? (Ephesians 4:27). Is there a particular situation with regard to your problem appetite that needs to be addressed? How will you go about protecting your life against Satan's advances?

_____

_____

_____

_____

3. List three benefits from your fellowship with other believers that brings you hope in your journey to fulfilling your appetites. (If you are not fellowshiping with other Christians, list three ways you will begin to practice this vital step to cultivating a divine appetite.)

_____

_____

_____

_____

4. Ask God to help you notice where you can be used and find purpose through service. If you can't think of these opportunities on your own, talk to your pastor or look into volunteering for a local cause that would share the love of Christ with others.

_____

_____

_____

Chapter 10: The Surrendered Life

1. Would you define your spiritual life as a "surrender"? Why or why not? What is holding you back from this necessary step?

_____

_____

_____

_____

2. Are you in regular communication with the Father by praying to Him and reading His Word so that you can grow spiritually as you are being pruned through temptation and struggle? Study Philippians 4:4–9 and reflect on God's assurances for His children.

_____

_____

_____

3. Read James 1:2–4 and Romans 8:28. How has God used the problem appetite in your life to bring spiritual growth? How are you experiencing greater Christ-likeness as a result of this journey?

_____

_____

_____

4. What is your chief ambition in life? Do you long for physical riches or security? To be admired? Or do you seek a life surrendered to Christ? Is it possible to seek earthly things and be surrendered? Back up your answer with Scripture.

_____

_____

_____

_____

❧

I have fought the good fight, I have finished the race, I have kept the faith. Now there is in store for me the crown of righteousness, which the Lord, the righteous Judge, will award to me on that day—and not only to me, but also to all who have longed for his appearing.

—2 Timothy 4:7–8

ENDNOTES

Chapter 1: The Quest for Fulfillment

1. Information regarding these celebrities came from: "Morbid curiosity: Celebrity tombstones across America." See http://site 33134.dellhost.com.
2. Bob Buford, *Finishing Well* (Nashville, TN: Integrity Publishers, 2004), n/a.

Chapter 2: What God Intended

1. *Webster's New World Dictionary of the American Language*, ed. David Guralnik (New York: Warner Books, 1984), s.v. "Subdue."

Chapter 3: The Choice Factor

1. Drug and Alcohol Addiction Information, "Pleasure Center Pathways." See http://www.egetgoing.com/Drug/5_5_3.asp.
    Kathleen McGowan, "The Biology of . . . Appetite," *Discover* 23 no. 9 (September 2002). See http://www.discover.com/sept_02/featbiology.html.
    Medical-Net Information Management Group, "Fat hormone linked to brain's pleasure center," Reuters Health (2000). See http://www.mnimg.com/Articles.
2. David Sper, ed. *Designed for Desire* (Grand Rapids, MI: RBC Ministries, 1993). Also see http://www.gospelcom.net/rbc/ds/cb932/cb932.html.
3. Harry W. Schaumburg, *False Intimacy: Understanding the Struggle of Sexual Addiction* (Colorado Springs, CO: NavPress, 1992), 60.
4. "Self-Indulgence," *Forerunner* (March-April 2001), 1. See http://bibletools.org.
5. John Piper, *Desiring God* (Sisters, OR.: Multnomah Press, 1986), 77.
6. C. S. Lewis, *The Weight of Glory* (San Francisco, CA: Harper, 2001), 1–2.
7. Stephen Apthorp, *Alcohol and Substance Abuse: A Clergy Handbook* (Wilton, CT: Morehouse-Barlow, 1985), 158–62.
8. Jeff Vanvonderen, *Good News for the Chemically Dependent and Those Who Love Them* (Minneapolis, MN: Bethany House Publishers, 1991), 40.
9. Ibid., 40–42.

ENDNOTES

Chapter 4: How Change Begins

1. Stephen Arterburn and David Stoop, *Seven Keys to Spiritual Renewal* (Wheaton, IL: Tyndale House Publishers, 1998), 74.
2. Stephen Arterburn, *Addicted to Love* (Ann Arbor, Mich.: Servant Publications, 1991), 142–43.
3. "Healthy Reasons to Have a Pet." See http://www.deltasociety.org/dsc020.html.
4. Karen Allen, "The Healthy Pleasure of Their Company: Companion Animals and Human Health." See http://www.deltasociety. org/dsz001.html.

Chapter 5: Introduction to Influences

1. Colette Dowling, *You Mean I Don't Have to Feel This Way?* (New York: Bantam Books, 1993), 88.
2. Stephen Apthorp, *Alcohol and Substance Abuse: A Clergy Handbook* (Wilton, CT: Morehouse-Barlow, 1985), 154.
3. "Control of our food intake is the basis behind successful weight loss". See http://www.weightlossfor all.com/food_intake.html.
4. "Coping with Food Cravings" (July/August 1991); http://www.primusweb.com/fitnesspartner/library/nutrition/cravings.html.
5. Stephen Arterburn, *Addicted to Love* (Ann Arbor, Mich.: Servant Publications, 1991), 68.
6. *Diagnostic & Statistical Manual of Mental Disorders: Fourth Edition* (Washington, D.C.: American Psychiatric Association, 1994).
7. Drug and Alcohol Addiction Information, "Gambling Addiction." See http://www.egetgoing.com/Drug/5_8_4.asp.
   Drug and Alcohol Addiction Information, "Pleasure Center Pathways." See http://www.egetgoing.com/Drug/5_5_3.asp.
   Medical-Net Information Management Group, "Fat hormone linked to brain's pleasure center," Reuters Health (2000). See http://www.mnimg.com/Articles.
8. "Are you addicted?" *USA Weekend* (September 26–28, 2003).
9. Paul Recer, "Social, Physical Pain Much the Same Inside Brain," *Newsleader* (October 10, 2003).

Chapter 6: Filling the Void (Times Eight)

1. Jeff Vanvonderen, *Good News for the Chemically Dependent and Those Who Love Them* (Minneapolis, MN: Bethany House Publishers, 1991), 18.
2. Stephen Arterburn, *Addicted to Love* (Ann Arbor, Mich.: Servant Publications, 1991), 173.
3. Ibid.
4. Vanvonderen, *Good News for the Chemically Dependent*, 92.

Chapter 7: Fruit in All Its Forms

1. *Webster's New World Dictionary of the American Language*, ed. David Guralnik (New York: Warner Books, 1984), s.v. "Fruit."
2. Adapted and developed from sermon outline "Practical Applications of What We Have Learned About Choices." See http://www.korrnet.org/karns/sermons/121999pm.html.

Chapter 8: New Pathways

1. American Obesity Association, "Obesity in the U.S." See http://www.obesity.org/subs/fastfacts/obesity_US.shtml.
2. *Webster's New World Dictionary of the American Language*, ed. David Guralnik (New York: Warner Books, 1984), s.v. "Excess."
3. Neal Barnard, M.D. "Breaking the Food Seduction," *Good Medicine* 12, no. 3 (Summer 2003), n.a.
4. David Sper, ed. *Designed for Desire* (Grand Rapids, Mich.: RBC Ministries, 1993). Also see http://www.gospelcom.net/rbc/ds/cb932/cb932.html.
5. "Comparisons of U.S. and Finnish Television Statistics." See http://www.uta.fi/FAST/US2/NOTES/finstats.html.
   Center for Media Education, "Children & Television: FAQ." See http://wwwlcme.org/children/kids_tv/c_and_t.html.
6. "Are you addicted?" *USA Weekend* (September 26–28, 2003), n.a.
7. American Bankruptcy Institute, "U.S. Bankruptcy Filings 1980-2002." See http://www.abiworld.org.
8. Jeanne Sahadi, "Debt: How Do You Stack Up?" *CNNMoney*. See http:money.cnn.com/2003/09/25/pf/millionaire/q_dedtstackup/index.html.
9. Ibid.
10. Justin Lahart, "Spending Our Way to Disaster," *CNNMoney*. See http://money.cnn.com/2003/10/02/markets/comsumerbubble/index.html.
11. Stress Management for Dummies, "Curbing Your Appetite for Stress-Inspired Eating." See http://cda.dummies.com/WileyCDA/DummiesArticle/id-973,subcat-EATING.html.
    "Controlling Appetite for Weight Loss." See http://jas.family.go.com.
    "When Stress Triggers Overeating." See http://www.24hourfitness.com.
    "Conquer Killer Cravings." See http://www.floridafitness.com/Fitness/Craving_killers.html.
    "Cravings, Overeating, and the Brain Connection." See website at: http://www.thedietchannel.com/weightloos5.html.
    "Coping with Food Cravings" (July/August 1991). See http://www.primusweb.com/fitnesspartner/library/nutrition/cravings.html.
12. Justin Lahart, "Spending Our Way to Disaster."

ENDNOTES

Chapter 9: Cultivating a Divine Appetite

1. Charles Allen, *God's Psychiatry* (Ada, Mich.: Fleming Revell, 1988), n.a.
7. Stephen Apthorp, *Alcohol and Substance Abuse: A Clergy Handbook* (Wilton, CT: Morehouse-Barlow, 1985), 7–8.

Chapter 10: The Surrendered Life

1. *Webster's New World Dictionary of the American Language*, ed. David Guralnik (New York: Warner Books, 1984), s.v. "Surrender."
2. Steven Arterburn and David Stoop, *Seven Keys to Spiritual Renewal* (Wheaton, IL: Tyndale House Publishers, 1998), 7–8.

Appendix : Twelve Steps to Successfully Feeding Your Appetites

1. "Practicing Self-Control." See http://www.personal-budget-planning-saving-money.com/selfcontrol.html.

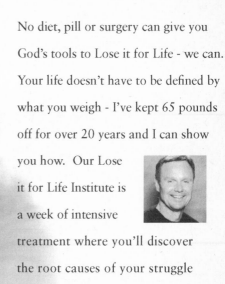